Escape from Singapore—1942

Escape from Singapore - 1942

The story of an incredible voyage through enemy waters

by
Ian Skidmore

Charles Scribner's Sons : New York

Copyright © 1973 by Ian Skidmore

This book published simultaneously in the
United States of America and in Canada –
Copyright under the Berne Convention

All rights reserved. No part of this book
may be reproduced in any form without the
permission of Charles Scribner's Sons

Printed in Great Britain

1 3 5 7 9 11 13 15 17 19 I/C 20 18 16 14 12 10 8 6 4 2

Library of Congress Catalog Card Number 73–13242
SBN 684–13638–4 (cloth)

Illustrations

		facing page
1.	The *Sederhana Djohanis*	104
2.	Keeping Watch	104
3.	Rowley about to climb the bowsprit	105
4.	The *Djohanis* catches the monsoon	105
5.	Waller, Gorham, Broome, Davis, Lind	120
6.	Loo Ngiap Soon and Jamal Bin Daim	120
7.	Alongside the *Anglo-Canadian*	121
8.	Brian Passmore	136
9.	Doc Davies	136
10.	The moment of rescue	136
11.	Spanton and Waller	137
12.	Davies and Campbell	137
13.	With the officers of the *Anglo-Canadian*	152
14.	The shelling of the *Sederhana Djohanis*	152
15.	The defiance of the *Sederhana Djohanis*	153
16.	Goodbye to the *Sederhana Djohanis*	153

Acknowledgements

My thanks are due to Colonel the Lord Langford of Bodrhyddan in North Wales, the 'Rowley' of the book, to Major D. C. A. Fraser, to Colonel L. E. C. Davies, the 'Doc' and to Major R. W. Kennard, M.C., for their help in compiling this record. They all gave unstintingly of their diaries, documents and their time to enable me to write the story of their adventure in Singapore and on the Indian Ocean and I am grateful to them. The detail of their recollection of events which happened to them nearly thirty years ago is not the smallest achievement of a group of very remarkable gentlemen.

My thanks also to Mrs Thea Nott without whose assistance this book would never have been completed and to my wife Celia without whom it would have been written in half the time yet not been nearly so much fun.

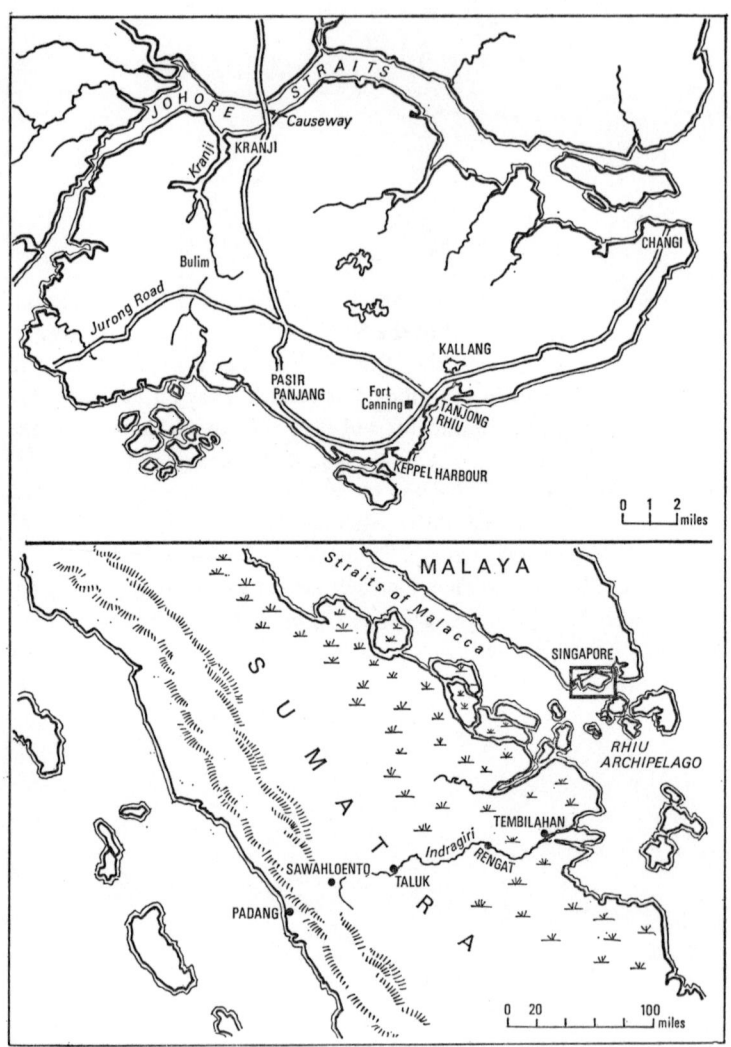

I

THE BATTLE was for the Island. The mainland had been lost and a thousand yards across the Johore Straits 70,000 war-hardened troops of the 25th Imperial Japanese Army waited impatiently for their orders for the final assault on the over-ripe colonial plum of Singapore.

From his war room in the tower of the Sultan of Johore's Palace in Johore Bahru, General Tomoyuki Yamashita waited no less impatiently for the plum to fall. He had earned his title 'The Tiger of Malaya'. In seventy-five days his soldiers had swept from the landing beaches at Singora and Pattani in Thailand and at Kota Bharu in Northern Malaya 500 miles through the Malay Peninsula to the shores of the Straits. Before an Asiatic audience he had roundly thrashed the White Imperialist to become, in the eyes of the Japanese man in the street, the living proof of the superiority of his race. Now he was knocking on the door of Singapore, the Gibraltar of the East and the bastion of Western supremacy in South East Asia.

Yamashita was a man who needed victory badly. Unwise political decisions had lost him the favour of the Emperor. Tojo, the Prime Minister, hated him and Yamashita feared assassination at his hands. His relations with his superiors in Southern Army were at breaking point. He had asked for five divisions for the campaign in Malaya and had been offered four. He had rejoined that he would capture Singapore with only three. And now he knew that his army was at full stretch.

With two of his divisional commanders, Takuro Matsui of the Fifth and Renya Mutaguchi of the Eighteenth, he was on good terms. But his relationship with Takuma Nishimura who commanded his third force, the Imperial Guards Division, was less happy. Nishimura was an ambitious man who smarted under Yamashita's frequent criticism of his troops. Colonel Masanobu Tsuji, his senior general staff officer, was a spy forced on Yamashita by Tojo.

So far he had been lucky. His first gamble, that he would get the bulk of his forces ashore in Thailand before the British overcame their diffidence about crossing into neutral territory had paid off. But his race through Malaya had brought supply problems. His generals had ammunition for only six days' fighting. His communication lines from Singora had virtually broken down and he knew that against the larger armies of the British, Australian and Indian forces he had not sufficient men to win a hand-to-hand battle in the streets of Singapore or even to break a determined defence on a wide front across the Island. Only a colossal bluff would bring him the victory he desperately needed; but he was a man who was prepared to play it.

In his canvas chair in the Sultan's palace Yamashita looked out at the shoreline of Singapore only a few thousand yards away and prepared for the gamble of his life. Despite the shortage of ammunition he ordered his artillery to maintain a barrage as though its supplies were unlimited. And he laid his final plans for the invasion.

Major Geoffrey Rowley-Conwy's problems were less complex and his quarters infinitely less comfortable. His anti-aircraft Battery of 3.7-inch heavy anti-aircraft guns, to which had recently been added sixteen 40-mm Bofors, had been ordered to form part of the general defence of the Island and their efforts had brought them to the attention of a Japanese mortar battery across the Straits. A professional soldier of twenty-nine, Rowley's heart was still with the horse-drawn field artillery regiment he had recently left. In the Gunner's hierarchy ack-ack guns were definitely below the salt and it was a touchy Rowley who chafed under the combined attentions of the mortars and the mosquitoes which bit every exposed inch of his body.

'Sarn't Major,' he called.

'Sir,' replied Battery Sergeant Major Arthur Sharman with the unjustified cheerfulness an N.C.O. somehow manages to inject into his voice at an officer's call.

'These blasted mortars. I think we'll have to try giving them a little of their own medicine over open sights.'

The B.S.M. grunted his agreement and the two men peered cautiously over the low crest in front of the guns, from where they could see the loping trajectory of the mortar bombs as they came towards them. As they watched, from the green heart of a palm tree on the enemy side, the surface of a binocular lens caught the sun and sent out an answering stab of light. Rowley's heart leapt.

'Got him,' he laughed. 'Over there, Sarn't Major. In the palm tree.'

The sergeant major had seen the flash and he was already scrambling down to set up the aiming posts which would give the predictor its line to the target over the low crest in front of them.

30 Battery was an anti-aircraft defence unit but the response to the new target was immediate. Gun barrels lowered and, only just clearing the immediate crest in front, steadied on their target. The range was read and the fuses set. Rowley watched the gently swaying palms each with its crop of Imperial Japanese fruit.

'Fire by order . . . one round salvo,' Rowley called to the gun position officer. 'Fire.' The guns answered. Their shells exploded in shattering airbursts just above the trees. A slow smile broke over the B.S.M.'s face as a mixed rain of palm fronds and Japanese soldiery cascaded in a confused hail on the mortars below leaving the trunks shivering and stark. The B.S.M. turned smartly and marched over to where Rowley was rubbing his hands.

'Every one a coconut, sir,' he reported.

'Delightful,' murmured Rowley. 'Thank you, Sarn't Major.'

Rowley's unorthodox action was received with less pleasure by his Brigadier in whose world anti-aircraft guns always fired upwards and never ever along. Rowley was summoned to the H.Q. of the Malayan Anti-Aircraft Defences.

'Absolute waste of ammunition,' his Brigade Major stormed. 'Your Battery is there for the purpose of helping to defend against attack by enemy bombers, not to take pot shots at individual soldiers. Good God, man, there won't be a shell left on the Island if this sort of behaviour gains currency. It's lucky for you the Brigadier's out having a look at the other batteries. He's absolutely mad with rage.'

Rowley apologised gracefully but he was unabashed. The mortar battery had not been firing at the Brigadier, he reflected, and it had been a highly successful action.

He decided not to pass on the Brigadier's reprimand to the Battery and they gloried in their unorthodox commanding officer. The story of the coconut shy was told and told again to the weary dispirited infantrymen who from time to time trudged past the Battery. In the wake of the beaten army refugees flooded on to the Island, too late to help build the defences that the G.O.C. had belatedly ordered; disastrously punctual to share the dwindling supplies of food and water which might otherwise have prolonged the campaign. On foot and cart, pedalling antique bicycles, marching bravely or staggering in exhaustion, the civilians and the soldiers, the white man and the brown man choked the roads as they assembled for the final act in the drama of Singapore.

But not all came in despair.

Rowley's Battery was once again in action at Ponggol against the formations of Japanese bombers which by now, almost unchallenged, were battering the Island into submission. The gunners' hands were blistered, their eyes red-rimmed from lack of sleep. Their nerves were taut and their faces streaked with the cordite smoke of their guns. Then one day as the B.S.M. was enjoying a cigarette at the edge of the gun-site and staring absently into the distance he saw a cloud of dust growing as it neared him. An unmilitary figure in a khaki drill was riding towards him on a travel-stained motor-cycle. As the sergeant major watched, the figure dismounted, dusted himself down and in a calm unhurried manner of a man approaching a stranger at a cocktail party advanced towards him. He was smilingly broadly and apparently unaware of the battle that was raging over his head. He carried a small suitcase.

Astonished, the Battery Sergeant Major watched him approach the gun position.

'Good morning,' said the stranger politely. 'I wonder if I could have a word with the boss.'

The sergeant major shuddered. 'The who?' he gasped.

The manager,' repeated the stranger pleasantly. 'I wonder if I could have a word with him.'

The sergeant major's reply was icy with contempt. 'Do you mean the Commanding Officer?'

'Yes, I suppose I do,' agreed the stranger. 'I wonder if you would tell him I'm here?'

Silently, yet with a precision which was in itself a reproof, B.S.M. Sharman marched off in the direction of Battery Headquarters.

At the sound of his B.S.M. coming smartly to attention Rowley looked up and returned the formal salute.

The B.S.M. looked stonily ahead.

'There is a gentleman to see you, sir; at least, I suppose he's a gentleman,' he said.

Geoffrey Rowley-Conwy was the heir to the Irish barony

of Langford; he was to inherit an estate in North Wales that his ancestors had defended against an assortment of foes since the early middle ages. When William the Conqueror landed in Britain a Conwy rode in his train. 400 years later another Conwy collected men from Rhuddlan and Dyserth and marched to Bosworth to help Henry Tudor win the throne of England. Such men are aware of the social niceties.

'Thank you, Sarn't Major,' he said. 'Would you show him in?'

'Sir,' said the B.S.M. with feeling.

On the gun site the stranger was watching the gun crews, engrossed. Douglas Fraser was a man with a grim purpose. He had come to Malaya before the war as a planter and become enchanted with the country. He held a private pilot's 'A' licence and a few months before war broke out he had transferred to the Malayan Volunteer Air Force from the Kedah Volunteer Force in which he was serving as a territorial. He was posted to Penang airport with the rank of Leading Aircraftman and flew in unarmed Tiger Moths without radio on daily reconnaissance sorties out to sea. When seven Jap Navy Zero fighters had swept down on the airfield at Penang, Fraser fought back with the airfields only armament, a Lewis gun set up next to the club house. He scored at least one direct hit and a fighter later crashed into the sea.

As he waited impatiently for the interview with Rowley-Conwy, Fraser glanced at his dusty motor-cycle and his mind went back over the days that had just passed. After the shattering news of the sinking of the *Prince of Wales* and the *Repulse* on 10 December, the R.A.F. was evacuated from their base near Penang and his flight of the M.V.A.F. took part in the general evacuation of the Island.

Fraser had returned to his rubber estate and collected his Triumph Tiger 100 motor-cycle. It was a wise decision. When his flight reached the mainland they were ordered to consolidate at Kallang airport on Singapore. It was a five-hundred-mile journey which Fraser made, thanks to his bike, in comparative comfort and at speed; but it was a journey that was nevertheless punctuated with incident. Time and again as the Japanese strafing from the air became too uncomfortable he had to skid to a halt and scramble into a roadside monsoon ditch. But he arrived safely at Kallang where the M.V.A.F. continued to fly until it was decided to ship the remaining planes to airfields in the Dutch East Indies. Fraser was given a rifle and ordered to fight with the infantry in the defence of the airfield. He waited for the coming of the Japanese impatiently. In off-duty hours he searched for his family and friends with whom he had lost touch and the news he learned was shattering. His twin brother who was serving as a sergeant in the Federated Malay States Volunteer Force had been killed during the retreat from Kuala Lumpur. There were Bofors guns surrounding the airfield and Fraser soon noticed that they were the only units showing any aggression. He made up his mind to join them and it was this decision which had brought him to Rowley's Battery.

Fraser's thoughts were broken by the voice of B.S.M. Sharman. 'Right. The Major will see you. Follow me.'

Fraser followed the B.S.M. to the headquarters building where Rowley was waiting. The circumstances were unusual, he looked forward with quiet pleasure to their solution and Fraser did not keep him waiting long. The courtesies observed he came briskly to the point.

'I'd like to join,' he said.

Rowley considered his visitor gravely. 'I see. Unfortunately it's not quite as easy as that. I mean there's a form to these things. I'm afraid you can't walk in and join His Majesty's Land Forces just like that. There are certain formalities to be observed. You'd better pop off to Singapore . . .'

Fraser interrupted him. 'I haven't time for all that. My brother has been killed, my plantation has been lost and I'd like to do something about it. It can't be too difficult, can it?

I mean, if I was just the chap who pushed the shell up the breech, I could do that, couldn't I? Surely it's not too difficult?' He told Rowley of his service with the M.A.V.F. and Rowley was impressed.

'Well, yes,' he admitted. 'You could learn the basics of that sort of gunnery in about ten minutes. But you see the problem is that I wouldn't be able to pay you anything. We can feed you and clothe you but not pay you. You're not on the roll, you see.'

Fraser saw immediately. 'Good heavens,' he said. 'I didn't expect to be paid. I just want to do something.'

There had been casualties, more were likely and Fraser's record was impressive. Rowley glanced at the sergeant major and suppressed a smile at the astonishment he saw on his face. He made up his mind.

'What did you say your name was . . . Fraser?'

'Sarn't Major, this is Gunner Fraser. I'm signing him on. Get him kitted out, will you? And fit him in on one of the guns as number four.'

B.S.M. Sharman fell back on the last line of defence available to senior N.C.O.s whose commanding officers have sent their orderly world spinning on its axis.

'Sir,' he said. And his tone of resignation was of one who neither questions nor complains nor necessarily approves: but as he marched his newest recruit to an astonished storeman he reflected that it would all make a nice replacement for the story of the coconut shy. And there was a bonus in the expression on the face of the storeman when the B.S.M. ordered, 'Get this fellow kitted out sharpish. The Major's signed him on.'

B.S.M. Sharman found it difficult to suppress his curiosity about his newest recruit. Fraser was that military rarity, a compulsive volunteer. At Kallang airport where a civil airlines Rapide made a daily flight to Sumatra, the B.S.M. learned, Fraser had volunteered to be its gunner. It had no armament of any kind so he had a hole cut into the top of the fuselage and a Lewis gun mounting screwed onto the frame.

Hanging half out of the plane Fraser was attached to the fuselage by a steel cable slotted into an anchorage on the floor and from this uncomfortable perch he searched the skies for the sophisticated Japanese Navy fighters. When he spotted them he had to reach back inside the plane for the heavy machine-gun, manhandle it on to the mounting and screw it into position before he was ready to fight back.

The long flights to Sumatra took from dawn to dusk at heights of never more than 500 feet and there was always the danger of being shot down by jumpy Dutch gunners. Yet somehow the plane and Fraser survived.

And now he had volunteered again.

'Do you know anything about guns?' the B.S.M. asked him.

'Nothing,' said Fraser happily, and the sergeant major swallowed.

'Well then,' he said, 'next time there's an alert you'd better just stand by and watch.'

'Delighted,' rejoined Fraser.

'And don't get in the bleeding way,' barked the B.S.M. in a last despairing attempt to control a situation which was slipping rapidly from his grasp.

The gun position to which Fraser was sent was a permanent site, part of the static defences built in peacetime. The gun emplacements were eight feet below ground level and the off-duty gun crews slept in palm-roofed wooden huts with slit trenches by their beds.

Fraser's first taste of action with the battery was against a formation of 27 Japanese bombers flying at 20,000 feet on a pattern bombing raid of the Island. He watched the gun crews bringing up shells, setting the fuses and handing them up to the guns for stacking into the loading trays. He admired the way the gunners worked, ignoring the bombs and mortar fire which exploded round their site and in their turn the gunners took to Fraser. In the days that followed they showed him the drill and congratulated him on the way he picked it up. For the first time for many days Fraser was entirely happy; but it was a brief idyll.

Too soon the battered remnants of the 2nd Argyll & Sutherland Highlanders were played on to the island by the only two pipers left to the battalion. They had fought a bitter rearguard action but now they marched in retreat across the causeway that linked Singapore with the mainland and scarcely had the last notes of the pipes died away when the causeway was breached by a demolition charge. But as with so much else in the battle of Singapore, it was not enough. The water that rushed into the gap was only four foot deep and when the invasion came, screaming Japanese breasted it at a run with their rifles over their heads.

Yamashita's major bombardment began on 5 February and went on for three days. Then, on 8 February, the enemy guns went silent and battalions of Japanese shock troops, veterans of the war with China, masters of seaborne landing and skilled in jungle warfare, made their way in a night attack over the straits in 200 collapsible boats and 100 larger landing craft.

That night 13,000 Japanese troops landed on the northwest coast of Singapore and another 10,000 joined them before dawn. Later when Nishimura's prickly self-esteem had been jolted by a cutting signal from Yamashita he consented to bring his own guards division into the battle. At least two more divisions were being held in reserve in the Kluang area of Johore but they were not needed. The fortress was about to be taken by an attacking force one third the size of the defenders' army. The militarily impossible was within a few days of becoming a reality.

Yamashita had correctly estimated that his troops were outnumbered three to one and he resolved on another gigantic bluff. Ironically it was one that General Allenby had used in Palestine with devastating effect in 1918. The Japanese built dummy camps opposite the Naval Base and convoys of lorries were ordered to move east every day and to move back westward again every night without lights. The impression on the British was of one vast eastward troop movement and the bluff worked.

Brigadier Ivan Simpson, the Chief Engineer of Malayan Command, had worked out the strategy of the Japanese correctly and had accordingly established dumps of engineer stores on the west of the causeway. The G.O.C., General A. E. Percival, was less perceptive and when news of the convoys of lorries reached him he ordered Simpson to move his dumps to the east.

The Chief Engineer had spent weeks establishing the dumps and equipping them with the ironmongery of war. He was appalled by the order, but he began the mammoth task of moving the mountains of mines, thousands of drums of petrol, booby traps and fencing posts. Soldiers humped the equipment on to lorries and moved them to the new sites. By 5 February they had just got everything in order when a fresh instruction was received. The General Staff were startled to observe that the Japanese invasion forces were massing almost opposite the original site of the dumps. The soldiers were ordered to move the dumps back but it was too late. Yamashita's bluff had succeeded magnificently.

By the time the Japanese did land the Australian 22nd Brigade who faced them had already suffered a day of shattering assault. From dawn on 8 February Japanese naval planes had been pattern-bombing their position. In the afternoon the forward defences were again subjected to a five-hour bombardment. Among other disasters it brought down the telephone lines by which the forward units were connected to their commanders. General Percival believed that the softening up by the guns would go on for three or four more days. It stopped the same night and the Japanese forward infantry began its attack.

Armoured landing craft carried the first troops but those that followed used any boat they could find and some were so eager for the fight they swam the mile across the straits with their arms and ammunition. Others made use of collapsible plywood rafts jointed with rubber which could be assembled in two minutes. Singly they could taken a dozen men. Roped in threes they could carry artillery.

The first wave of troops was all but wiped out by the Australian defenders but its place was taken by another and yet another wave until the Australians, by this time almost without ammunition, were finally swamped. The defence was hampered by darkness. Searchlights trained on the shore were never used on the orders of the General Staff who feared that the Japanese might shoot them out. Instead the enemy were able to capture them intact and operate them against the Allies.

The crossing was made on an eight-mile stretch and to the surprise of the Japanese the artillery bombardment they faced was slight. The Australian Commander Gordon Bennett had shared Percival's belief that the invasion would not begin for three days and in consequence no orders were issued for the gunners to put down concentrations on the creeks. By cutting the telephone wires the Japanese prevented news of the invasion reaching the guns and it was only when distress rockets were sent up by the Australian infantry that they began a bombardment. By then it was too late to be effective.

With only dark outlines as their targets or the sounds of the engines of the landing craft the task of the Australians was hopeless; yet they battled on. When their ammunition ran out they fought in the mangrove swamps with their bayonets. But in time they were overwhelmed and the main Japanese force established itself on the island in slightly less than an hour.

On the day of the landing Rowley was called before his

Colonel. As he saluted Rowley felt uneasy. The unorthodox Major and the regimentally minded Colonel were never in complete military harmony. Lt-Colonel Francis Hugonin looked at the untidy young Major who stood before him.

'I'm afraid I've got a pretty unpleasant job for you, Rowley,' he said. 'There is a G.L. Set on the Jurong Road and the Japanese are either near its site or they have overrun it. In either case it must be destroyed or brought back.'

G.L. sets were the forerunners of later and more sophisticated radar systems. So far only the British forces were equipped with them but Rowley had seen enough of the Japanese ability to copy machinery to know that it would not take their scientists long to reproduce the equipment and use it against the Allies. Yet the prospect of fighting through the Japanese advance to destroy it was not attractive.

At his own Battery H.Q. Rowley passed his orders to Sharman and to Sergeant Pearson. Sharman had been with Rowley for three years. He was stolid and dependable and would go wherever Rowley could lead. Pearson was a tough, reckless man who in peacetime had been one of Rowley's problems. He attracted trouble and had been up and down the ranks like a yo-yo; but he was a resourceful and imaginative soldier with a gift for leadership. Twelve gunners were picked for their ability with Lewis guns, rifles and small arms. For transport they had two Field Artillery 'Quads', soft-skinned vehicles with four-wheel drive and an open observation turret on the cab roof.

They left the gun position at dusk; the enemy were attacking on a front between the causeway and the River Kranji and once again, despite heavy losses, they had gained a footing. The 22nd Australian Brigade fighting in the Bulim area had been ordered to withdraw to a position on the right of the 6th/15th Brigade in the Kranji–Jurong line. In the confusion of the retreat they withdrew too far and the Japs poured through the gap in the line, driving the defenders before them.

It was against this sea of frightened and battered troops that Rowley's small convoy had to force its way up the Jurong road in search of the missing G.L. set. The nerves of the retreating soldiers were at breaking point. Rowley, arms on the turret rim of his truck, was reflectively smoking an evening pipe when a voice called out of the darkness: 'If you don't put out that bloody light I'll shoot it out.' It was not the moment for a discussion with a disembodied voice and Rowley knocked out his pipe resignedly.

He watched, sickened, as wild-eyed infantrymen, both white and brown, swept past him on foot and in trucks, rushing back down the road he had just travelled. Then a shout from his driver brought him with a jolt to his own problems.

'There's something blocking the road ahead,' the gunner told him. Rowley eased himself out of the turret and jumped down from the cab. Some way ahead in the dark he could make out the outline of a troop of 25-pounder field guns straggled across the road. His temper flared and striding up to the leading vehicle he found an officer peering uncertainly about him.

Rowley exploded: 'Do you realise you are blocking the whole bloody road?' he said. The young Gunner captain was equally short: 'Can't help that. I was told to rendezvous here and here I am.'

'Here?' said Rowley. 'In the middle of the road. Are you sure you've got the right place?'

The youngster was icily polite. 'And how can I be sure of that? I haven't got a map. Nobody's got a bloody map.' His voice shook. 'Would you believe it, Malaya Command have run out of maps. I'm trying to site a troop of field artillery in a strange country and they can't give me a bloody map. What a way to run a war.'

Rowley felt sympathy for the young Gunner. 'Take mine,' he said. 'I've been here for three years and I know the Island pretty well. I'll get you another from my N.C.O.'

Under a hooded torch the officer pored over the map. 'Hell,' he said after a moment. 'Wrong place, sorry.'

He shouted impatient orders. There was a grinding of gears and his troop got under way as Rowley scrambled back into his vehicle.

When at last the troop moved out it let the cork out of the bottle on the road. What had before been a river of soldiers became a flood. Many of the Island roads are single track and on each side there are monsoon ditches designed to drain away the heavy falls of rain. The ditches are wide enough and deep enough to take a lorry and on that night many did. Time and again Rowley and his gunners watched in astonishment as the retreating soldiers leaped out of stalled trucks, rocked them off their balance and with a final heave toppled them into the ditches while their passengers scrambled on to the vehicle following and continued their headlong flight. Indian soldiers had cast away their boots, the better to run, and barefoot they were trotting in a loose mob, chattering hysterically.

From his turret in the leading vehicle Rowley was beginning to despair of ever finding the G.L. set when he spotted an officer and a signaller crouched at the road side under a palm-roofed hut. Rowley ordered the drivers to take the Quads on to a rubber estate road nearby and to park them under guard. Then, with a small party, he climbed down from the transport and pushed his way through the mob of soldiers to the shelter.

Under his palm roof the officer, a Brigade Major in the Indian infantry, was writing out, by the light of a hooded lantern, orders to Battalion Commanders for the morning's counter-attack. Rowley waited for him to pause and then introduced himself. He said: 'I've been ordered to destroy a G.L. set. Do you know where the Japs are?'

The Major waved his pencil at the plantation. 'What a G.L. set is I wouldn't know,' he said, 'but the Japanese forward troops are about 400 yards in front in those trees.' Rowley was about to reply when out of the darkness a second voice broke in. It said: 'I know what it is, Sir. I'm Sergeant Wate. I was in charge of it and I destroyed it. I've brought the valves and some parts with me.'

A figure stepped out of the gloom with the gleaming valves in his hand. Rowley took them and tried not to show his relief but his heart was pounding as he returned and gave the order to head back down the Jurong Road to camp. There, the valves handed over and Sergeant Wate filled with tea and stew, Colonel Hugonin and Rowley chatted generally about the war. Rowley was optimistic until Hugonin, like a schoolmaster reproving a pupil, said, 'You don't seem to realise, Rowley, we're rats in a trap.'

The words hit Rowley and he felt appalled. Until that moment the idea that Singapore could be lost to the Japanese had never entered his head. Like most of the regular soldiers on the Island he had believed fully in the myth of its impregnability. Now he wondered how many of his senior officers shared the Colonel's view.

On the 10th Churchill had signalled General Sir Archibald Wavell to express his dismay that Percival was being beaten when he had under his command more men than the Japanese had in the whole of Malaya. The Prime Minister took the view that the Japanese should be destroyed in one wellcontested battle, and he ordered that there must be no thought of saving the troops or of sparing the civilian population.

He ended: 'Commanders and Senior officers should die with their troops. The honour of the British Empire and the British Army is at stake. I rely on you to show no mercy to weakness in any form.'

Wavell was by this time in hospital recovering from a fall on the Singapore quay in which he had broken two bones in his back. His signal to Percival was more realistic than the one he had himself received.

It ended: 'When everything humanly possible has been

done some bold and determined personnel may be able to escape by small craft and make their way south to Sumatra and the islands.'

This last signal, had he known of its existence, would have brought Rowley some comfort in the days ahead. Its sentiment chimed happily with an idea that was beginning to form in his head.

Subsequently his battery had been moved to Pasir Panjang in the south-west of the Island. Here high-flying bombers were replaced by low-flying fighters and dive bombers. The 3·7-inch heavy ack-ack guns were useless in the role for which they were originally designed and the battery turned to a new kind of fighting, firing over open sights at the low-flying planes. Under instruction from more experienced men Fraser learned to set the fuses of the shells so that they exploded shortly after leaving the muzzle of the gun. It reminded him of clay pigeon shooting of pre-war days but he wished that the heavy ack-ack guns could be manoeuvred with the ease of a shot-gun.

Yamashita left his forward Headquarters in Malaya and with his staff he crowded on to a small barge and crossed the Straits of Johore. Colonel Tsuji was one of the first ashore. He felt something moving under his feet. Alarmed he switched on his torch. His hoot of delight startled his companions. They followed the beam of his torch and saw the frightened face of a white soldier blinking in its glare. The first Japanese assault force to establish a beach-head had moved on so quickly there was no time to marshal their prisoners. Instead they had roped them and thrown them to the ground and now the Japanese General Staff were walking over their bodies. The superstitious Yamashita appreciated the symbolism.

The island's main seaward defences began around Changi in the east. The line of heavy guns in fixed emplacements, a few concrete pill boxes, anti-boat and anti-tank obstacles, land mines and barbed-wire fences stretched to the Naval Base in the north-east and then south-west to Singapore City but Yamashita invaded in the more vulnerable north and west of the island where the defences were negligible.

General Wavell had been worried about the lack of defences on the north of the island and had ordered they should be built at once. But it was too late. On his return from his last visit to the island he had signalled to Churchill.

His message read: 'The battle for Singapore is not going well. The Japanese with their usual infiltration tactics are getting on much more rapidly than they should.' He criticized the morale of the troops and went on: 'The chief troubles are a lack of training in some of the reinforcing troops and an inferiority complex which bold and skilful Japanese tactics and their skill in the air have caused...'

The situation was to worsen with bewildering speed. By the 13th the British line was stretched along a 28-mile perimeter covering Singapore City where the streets were choked with the retreating army. Vehicles were abandoned and columns of lost troops waited dispiritedly to be claimed. Looting was by now widespread and the pavements were covered with the ripped packets of thousands of cigarettes. Women clutched stolen food as they hurried through the streets and even the children joined in the pillage.

Yamashita was not without worries of his own. His Chief Supply Officer, Colonel Ikanti, warned him that shortages of petrol and artillery ammunition made a siege impossible. The line of communications from Japan via Singora to Singapore had broken down and Yamashita lacked the men to fight for the city street by street.

Percival too was concerned at the plight of his army. He signalled to Wavell: 'The enemy are now within 5,000 yards of the seafront which brings the whole of Singapore within field artillery range. We are also in danger of being driven off water and food supplies. In the opinion of commanders the troops already committed are too exhausted either to withstand strong attack or to launch a counter attack.' The signal ploughed dispiritedly on: 'There must come a time when in the interests of the troops and the civilian population further bloodshed will serve no useful purpose.' He asked for the power which would give him the right to surrender, but the request was refused. Wavell ordered his G.O.C. to fight on until his men could fight no more.

Rowley's battery once again had orders to fall back, this time to Alexandra just west of the City. During a patrol of the surrounding district Rowley came across the abandoned married quarter of a Brigadier at Number 4, Royal Road. Applying his personal theories that it costs only a little more to travel first class and that any fool can be uncomfortable, Rowley collected his kit from his own married quarter in Changi and moved into the Brigadier's empty house.

He established his battery headquarters in the drawing-room and used what had been the child's night nursery as his bedroom. It was there that he caught sight of a map pinned to the wall. It was a page from a school atlas and the scale was small. Rangoon and Sydney were shown on the same sheet. But it also showed the vital small islands off Singapore and the sea passage to Sumatra. Carefully Rowley unpinned it, folded it and buttoned it into the pocket of his shirt. If he did escape it would be better to have his inadequate map than none at all.

The days passed and the strain on his gunners was beginning to show. One night he was awakened by shots just outside the house. He struggled awake and stumbled down into the hall. In the doorway Sharman had a half-nelson on a flushed and arrogant gunner. He looked up when he heard Rowley.

'Drunk on guard, Sir,' he reported. 'I found him sitting down loosing off his rifle.'

By an earlier order of the General Officer Commanding one and a half million bottles of spirits had been poured away to keep them from the Japs. Some of the gutters of the city were flooded with drink and the soldier had drunk himself into a stupor.

The next morning Rowley paraded his battery. As they fell in before him he drew his personal weapon, a .32 Colt automatic, and weighed it in his hand.

The speech he made was short but the effect was devastating. Holding the gun lightly Rowley told his men: 'When the chips are down there are only two kinds of punishment, corporal or capital. The next man who takes a drink on sentry duty will be dealt with in the only way which is available to me.'

His major problem was drinking water and he ordered his gunners to fill the bath tubs in every empty house in the vicinity of the gun site. The bathroom doors were locked and the keys handed over to a senior N.C.O.

Rowley had two dogs, Yellow, a cocker spaniel, and a border terrier, Kelso, who shivered in terror at the whine and crash of the bombs. Kelso had always been frightened by the frequent Malayan thunderstorms. Rowley called to Micklethwaite, the battery clerk. He told him to go into the garden and dig a small grave. When it was ready he took out his revolver and led Kelso out of the house. Moments later Micklethwaite heard a shot. In the stables down the hill at the rear of the house were two old racehorses, Brownhill and Jarrahwood which Rowley had used as hacks. For a moment he stood beside the grave of his dog and then he turned for the stables and shot both the horses.

That night the road at the foot of the gun site caught fire. The tar surface, softened by the tropic sun, was ignited by a shell and flames danced along a thirty yard stretch of the road. The blazing road proved a special hazard for the drivers who brought supplies of ammunition. A spark from one of the flames catching a petrol tank could have blown the convoy to atoms but the drivers pointed their trucks at the fire and accelerated through the wall of flame. Luckily there were no casualties.

That night, as the sounds of small arms fire intensified Rowley heard trucks outside the battery headquarters. He hurried out to investigate and was relieved to see British troops jumping out. A company of the Loyal Regiment had withdrawn on to the gun site. But his relief faded as he watched the Company Commander giving his orders. The man was dropping. Four times, as he went through the plans for their deployment, he fell asleep on his feet and had to be nudged awake. Rowley wondered what sort of defence these weary men could possibly make, but the next morning, as mortar bombs crashed through his headquarters, he was ordered to destroy his heavy guns and move back with his remaining Bofors.

The battery's next position was, by a coincidence, at Fraser's earlier posting, Kallang, the last airport on the Island to remain operational. Once again baths in empty houses were filled, their doors locked and ration stores set up. Rowley was worried about his men; some of them were near breaking point. Before they left Alexandra Sharman had taken him to a slit trench.

In the bottom a young gunner was cowering; he was crying.

'What are you doing down there?' asked Rowley.

The gunner looked up sobbing: 'I can't come out, sir. I just can't stand it any more,' he said.

Rowley reached into the trench and dragged the soldier out by the front of his shirt. He slapped his face: 'You've got to stand it,' he told him. 'We've all got to stand it. There isn't anything else we can do.'

As he watched his battery digging itself in Rowley wondered how many others were near the edge. They were shortly to be tested. The slit trench for the administrative staff had just been dug when a broad formation of 36 bombers swept over the field. At 12,000 feet they were out of range of the

Bofors which by this time were all the weapons the battery had left. The invariable signal for bombing to begin, a short burst of machine-gun fire from the leading plane, ripped the sky above them.

In the clear air the men on the ground saw the bomb doors open, the bombs turn over and over, straighten and then settle in their downward flight to the ground below. There was a clattering and whining which grew into a harsh scream, then the shattering, ear-splitting explosion as the bombs crashed into the ground all round the slit trenches. The earth shook as the bombs continued to fall and the men sweated, their eyes, mouths and ears filled with dust and sand.

At last the raid ended and Rowley straightened up, peering over the rim of his trench. Dust was everywhere but he heard laughter and shouts of relief as he climbed out and began a tour of inspection. In the last gun pit he visited, a gunner looked up at him, grinning broadly. 'We knew we'd be all right, sir,' he told Rowley confidently. 'We had the Padre with us.' As he walked away Rowley ached for a scrap of the same kind of faith.

It was the last of the raids on the airport. Fighter defence over Singapore was no more and the Japanese fliers turned their attention to more worthwhile targets. There was nothing to be gained by damaging airfields they might soon occupy and in the temporary peace that followed Rowley took stock of his surroundings.

On Tanjong Rhu, a narrow spit of land between Kallang and Singapore city, he could make out the shells of bomb-damaged boat-building sheds. He hurried over to inspect them, and saw to his delight, moored a little way out from the sea wall an undamaged thirty-foot diesel launch. He could just make out the name on her bow, *Joan*. She was a sturdy little off-shore cruiser and beyond her a line of junks rode at anchor. With the aid of the page from the school atlas he had torn from the nursery wall, a small group of men could edge through the islands in the *Joan* and one of the junks. With luck and a calm sea they could reach Dutch Sumatra, sixty miles across the water.

Rowley now had the map, he had the plan, he had the boats and limping crossly round his battery, chafing at his inactivity, was the man to help him carry out his design.

2

CAPTAIN BOBBY KENNARD of the Argyll and Sutherland Highlanders was staying with Rowley, recovering from a bullet wound in the groin. They had been at Marlborough together. When Rowley moved to the Brigadier's bungalow Bobby had limped after him and when Rowley moved to Kallang, Bobby went too.

He had been wounded commanding 'C' Company of his regiment in a 'stopping' action against the Japanese in the early days of the Malaya campaign on the Grik Road. In holding up the Japanese advance his company lost fifty per cent of its men. After he was hit Bobby passed out and when he regained consciousness the battalion had gone. He tried to stand but with a serious wound in the groin his legs would not support him. He was trapped and helpless. Lying some distance from the road he could see through the undergrowth the Rising Sun on the sides of army trucks as they trundled past filled with troops. Trained as he was in jungle fighting, he was amazed at the noise the Japanese soldiers made as, first in the trucks and then on long processions of bicycles, they passed his hiding place. Even in his agony he was able to criticise the support troops as indifferent soldiers, whatever the advance battalions had been like. It was a thought that gave him strength as slowly, painfully, he raised himself to his knees and began to crawl.

For three days he crawled through the jungle on his hands and knees. His kneecaps became torn and poisoned by the jungle undergrowth but he crawled on. Once as he hid, biting his lips against the pain, in a bank covered in giant rhubarb, a Japanese Company marched within a yard of his face.

Eventually he reached the Perak river. Too weak almost to move but realising the river might take him south-west, he slipped into the water and grabbed a log as it passed him. He drifted downstream in a semi-daze until he was jolted back into life by the sound of light automatic fire. Plumes of water spouted round his log. Expecting to see a Jap he turned his head and then let out a shout of protest. He was being fired at by his own side. The man with the rifle was an Indian soldier. Furiously Bobby lifted an arm and shook his fist. The Indian saw the white skin, leapt into the river and Bobby was pulled to safety.

And after all that, Bobby thought bitterly as he sat watching Rowley's battery at work, here he was again with a very good chance of going into the Japanese bag. It was too bad. At home he had a wife he was longing to see and to become a prisoner was unthinkable. He decided to escape.

Bobby Kennard was a punctilious man. First he sought out his Brigadier, Archie Paris, and only when his decision had been approved and permission given to a wounded man, did he make his next move.

He packed his shaving kit and a change of clothing in his Hong Kong basket, a wicker-work suitcase favoured in the tropics. He said his goodbyes to the few of his friends who were left and set off back to Rowley's new battery headquarters at Kallang. It was an awesome journey. The sky over Singapore was dark and heavy with the smoke from burning oil. It turned white uniforms black and lay sharp on the dry tongues of the soldiers he passed. Sweat carved channels down their tired and sooty faces. Poured into the sea and set alight the oil from the storage tanks round the island might have built a wall of flame to delay the Japanese landing. But the decisions made in the dying days of Singapore were often hasty and ill-advised. Instead the oil was set alight in the tanks and the great black cloud lowered morale in the city even further.

The oily dust fell everywhere, on hungry stragglers searching for their units, on armed deserters who roamed the streets searching for loot, on cowardly and fear-crazed men fighting their way at the point of a gun or bayonet, pushing women and children aside, up the gangplanks of ships assembled to take civilians to safety. In the city the raids were taking a heavy toll. There were no underground shelters and few on the surface. People were dying at the rate of two thousand a day.

In two months the army which now waited for the final battle had retreated over four hundred miles. Fighters, bombers and the abstract death of long range guns had taken their various tolls. Morale, never high in Singapore, plummeted and in many the will to fight died completely.

More than three-quarters of the warehouses on the docks had been destroyed and the godowns in Keppel Harbour were smashed to matchwood. The £65,000,000 Naval Base had been abandoned, the great floating dock which had been towed from England was scuttled, the pumping machinery destroyed and Singapore's main line of defence, the giant coast defence guns were destroyed or dismantled.

Outside the city a queue of Europeans, three-quarters of a mile long, waited all one night outside the bungalow of a shipping manager on the top of Cluny Hill. It was a queue of despair and those who were successful in their wait for tickets were in most cases merely buying a few extra days of life. Out of fifty ships which sailed from Singapore packed with evacuees, forty were sunk within days of casting off. There were few survivors.

The great stone steps which led up to the municipal buildings were packed with Australian soldiers. The General Hospital was crammed with wounded and the staff worked in blood-soaked uniforms. The gutters ran with the spirits and the beer that had been poured away to prevent the Japanese from drinking themselves into a blood lust, as they had already done in Hong Kong.

Under the black oil clouds, darker clouds of pessimism were growing by the hour. Pessimism made Rowley angry and he chafed as he sensed it in the Island round him. He came to the door of his battery H.Q. at the sound of a motor bike and watched impatiently as a despatch rider made his way up the dusty road towards him. He groaned when he read the signal the man had brought.

Kennard had reached the battery by now and was walking towards him. 'Bobby,' he called: 'Have we done anything wrong recently?'

Bobby shook his head slowly. 'Not that I can think of,' he said. 'Certainly no more than we usually do. Why?'

'I've been summoned to Fort Canning and that means trouble of some kind.'

Rowley decided to take his friend into his confidence. 'Look, Bobby,' he said, 'I don't think there is much future in this and frankly I'm not proposing to stay. How about you?'

Bobby grinned. 'When do we leave?' he asked. 'As you see, I'm packed already.' He lifted the basket.

Briefly Rowley told Bobby of his plan to take the *Joan* and one of the Chinese junks lying at anchor in the Outer Roads a mile off the harbour and escape to Sumatra. Bobby was enthusiastic and the two men climbed into a 15 cwt truck and drove from the battery on the east side of Kallang airport to the slipway of Thorneycroft's boat yards. About a mile out they saw the line of junks rocking in the tideway. Rowley suggested that Bobby should arrange a boarding party and they agreed the junk was to be re-named *Conwy Castle*, after the castle near Rowley's home in North Wales which one of his ancestors had owned. In addition Bobby took over the task of provisioning and watering the craft and making all ready for the evacuation.

Both men realized the delicacy of the situation. If he left without getting the approval of a senior officer Rowley might technically be held to have deserted. If he stayed until after the surrender when his right to escape was protected by military law it might be too late to mount the operation. The timing would have to be exact.

As Sergeant Pearson drove up in the Quad which was to take him to Fort Canning, Rowley turned to Bobby. 'I'll try to find out all I can and I'll take a second Quad with me,' he told him. 'It's bound to be a mass counter-attack or a surrender; if I find that a pack-up is planned I'll send a message back to you which will include the words "Conwy Castle". That will be your signal to get things moving. You take the *Joan* and I'll take the junk.'

Bobby protested that the man who had the *Joan* would have the best chance of success and tried to persuade Rowley to take the launch. The idea had been Rowley's he argued, but Rowley smiled and shook his head.

'You take the *Joan*,' he said as he climbed into the vehicle, 'and don't hang about too long after you get my message.'

It was his second drive of the day. Earlier the battery had shot down a Japanese fighter which crashed in Singapore's red light district on Lavender Road and Rowley had been driven out to inspect the wreckage. The plane was scattered over a very wide area as though it had hit a building as it crashed. It looked small on the ground. There were sections of wings and fuselage and a crater where the engine had buried itself and at their feet they saw the forearm and hand of the dead pilot. The gunner driver turned the limb over with his boot and looked at it.

'Bloody dirty fingernails, sir,' was his only comment.

Not for the first time, as he drove to Fort Canning, Rowley was grateful for the turret in the roof of the cab of his Quad. A man could stand on the passenger seat and, with his head and shoulders through the turret, command an extensive field of fire with a Thompson sub-machine gun. The Quad had a soft top off which grenades would bounce harmlessly into the road and a four-wheel drive which was to prove invaluable on the journey to the Fortress H.Q.

Rowley had been warned to keep a special watch for anyone wearing a Malayan Ambulance Service armband. It was believed the Japanese had infiltrated the service and were sniping at anyone they saw. From time to time the vehicles were fired on with small arms but the range was long and his little convoy reached the centre of the town safely.

He was appalled at the sight that greeted him. In Victoria Road there were only craters and great piles of rubble where once there had been houses and hotels. It was as though someone had taken a house, shaken it and dumped it in untidy heaps on the road. In parts the rubble was piled ten feet high and the Quads had to engage four-wheel drive to get over the broken masonry. There were tram cars lying on their side and blue sparks of live electricity leapt from the broken overhead wires. As the Quads edged forward they caught the dangling wires and the men started at the twang of broken wire and the flashes of flame.

By this time the bombing had ceased and the streets were empty and menacingly silent. The only sound was the whining of the four-wheel drive of the Quads as they climbed over the rubble and the crackle of occasional rifle shots. The dead lay in the streets, shot down by fighter pilots as they ran out of their homes at the sound of the bombing or killed by bombs or by shells from the long range guns. The early days of the bombardment had began almost formally on 4 February with the shelling of Government House and since then the bodies of victims had been piled in trucks and emptied into mass graves between raids. But no one collected the corpses now. Cars, abandoned by their owners and hit by stray bullets, blazed untended. Dogs and cats shivered with fear and scuttled from empty doorways.

It was an unnerving drive across the ruined city and the gunners in the Quads were relieved when they reached the huge doors of Fort Canning and the underground battle headquarters of the armed services in Singapore.

Rowley had thought he might have been ordered to the fort to be told that a last counter-attack was to be mounted. There were only two alternatives that he could see: either every single soldier, including those in the heavy administrative tail, would join in a mass counter-attack in a final bid to beat the Japanese or there would be a surrender. He was not to know that at a conference that morning, Black Sunday, 15 February, General Percival had agreed to surrender the Island to the enemy.

In his underground office in the stale air and gloom Percival had penned his last message as G.O.C. to his troops.

'... In a few days we shall have neither food nor petrol, many types of ammunition are short and the water supply upon which the vast civil population and many of the fighting forces are dependent threatens to fail. This situation has been brought about partly by being driven off the dumps and partly by hostile air and artillery action. Without these necessities of war we cannot carry on...'

As long ago as 15 January General Wavell had warned Churchill that Singapore was not in a position to defend itself. Churchill's answer had been a slashing condemnation of the slipshod preparations for war by the Island's defenders. He told Wavell that it was incredible that a defence plan to dominate the mainland, an elementary peacetime provision, did not exist in a fortress that had been twenty years in building. He criticised reliance on the seaward batteries at the Naval Base and he added:

'I warn you that this will be one of the greatest scandals that could possibly be exposed.'

In his office in the heat and growing dark Percival waited for the scandal to break over his head.

The atmosphere in the Royal Artillery Branch was scarcely

lighter. As he pushed open the doors Rowley saw that every battery commander he had ever met on the Island had found his way into the lecture hall. There were not enough chairs and officers were sitting propped against the walls or lying on the floor. Many were exhausted. Others were chatting quietly and the luckier ones had bottles of beer which they shared with their friends.

Among them Rowley saw one face he knew well. Major Freddie Ievers had been his battery commander when Rowley was a captain. In Southern Ireland they had been in the same brigade and when Rowley first arrived in Singapore he stayed at the Ievers' home until he found a flat.

He pushed his way through the crowd until he reached Ievers.

'Well, Jeeves,' he said. 'What's the form? Do we fight or is it a surrender?'

Ievers shook his head. 'I know the form but I'm not allowed to tell you,' he said. 'I'm sorry.' Rowley nodded and after a short talk moved on to confront his regimental adjutant, Peter Ligertwood. From him he learnt the discomforting news that his commanding officer was in hospital but nothing of future plans. He was beginning to get desperate for information when he saw an old friend who he thought would tell him what he wanted to know. Major Willie Hargreaves had served under him as a captain before he got a battery of his own. Hargreaves smiled a greeting but was unwilling to answer his questions. Rowley had little time for subtleties.

'Look here, Willie,' he said, 'I helped to put that crown on your shoulders and now you can do something for me. One of two things is going to happen. Either there is going to be a counter-attack or a surrender and if it's a pack-up I'm not staying. I've got a junk in the outer roads. All I'm asking is this—would you advise me to board the junk?'

Willie looked at the slight figure before him.

'If I were you,' he said, 'I'd board it as quickly as you can after half past eight this evening.'

'Thank you,' said Rowley. 'The password is "Conwy Castle" and there is a place aboard for you if you want it.'

He nodded and made his way back to the adjutant. 'Peter,' he said, 'I've discovered your little secret and I'm not staying.'

'You've got to,' the adjutant replied. 'You must attend this conference.'

Rowley was firm. 'I don't think I will, thank you. If I'm right it's only a conference about how to surrender and at the moment I'm more concerned about how to escape. There is a junk in the outer roads and we're going to board it. The password is "Conwy Castle" and we'd be delighted to see the Colonel and yourself.'

The adjutant shook his head. 'The Colonel can't make it and I certainly can't leave the Colonel.'

'The offer is there,' said Rowley. 'We hope to be off about three in the morning if you change your mind.'

His excitement mounted as he hurried back down the long concrete passages to the entrance where his Quads were still parked under a group of trees. In the failing light he scribbled a note on a message-pad—'Occupy Conwy Castle immediately'—and handed it up to the driver of the second Quad. 'Take that back to the battery and give it personally to Captain Kennard,' he told the man. 'Sergeant Pearson, you wait here for me,' he called to the other truck and he hurried back through the doors of the headquarters.

Rowley knew that the approaches to Singapore were heavily mined and it was essential that he should have a plan of the minefields if he was to get his boats to safety. He made his way to the Coast Defence Artillery offices where the Brigade Major was an acquaintance.

There was no time to waste. In a low voice Rowley said, 'I understand there's going to be surrender, so I'm off. Have you got a map of the minefields?'

The Brigade Major shook his head. 'There is only one,' he

said, 'and that's on the wall in the Brigadier's office.' He paused. 'You can't take it but I don't see why you shouldn't copy it.'

He led Rowley into an office where the Brigadier was talking intently with three other men. The Brigadier hardly looked up to return Rowley's salute and the B.M. pointed to the wall where a large chart hung. Rowley copied it on a sheet of foolscap he had picked off a desk, sketching in as many stretches of the coast as time allowed.

On his way out he thanked the Brigade Major and offered him a place on the *Conwy Castle*. 'Sorry,' he answered ruefully, 'I can't leave the Brigadier.'

Outside the headquarters, Pearson was waiting in the Quad with a gunner behind the wheel and two more with loaded rifles in the back of the vehicle. He was standing on the passenger seat with his head and shoulders sticking out of the turret. His Thompson rested on the cab roof.

It was dark by now and the journey back from Fort Canning without lights and in low gear was even more nerve-racking than the earlier journey had been. The silence was oppressive and the darkness intense. There was no moon and smoke from the oil tanks was still choking the Island. By now the shelling had stopped and there were no aircraft overhead. Resistance was dying.

The Quad's windscreen had been poked out to give a clean field of fire from the cab and the two gunners in the rear were ready to leap out at the first sign of attack. But they arrived at their battery without incident. On the landward end of the narrow strip which led to the boatyard Rowley's Troop Captain, John Purvis, had put up a road block. The soldiers who manned it waved Rowley's vehicle through.

At the gun site he found that Bobby had been busy from the moment he had received the signal to occupy the junk. He had boarded one and had provisioned her for 48 hours. It had been a complicated operation, especially after dark. The launch could not get alongside the sea wall so he left it moored to a buoy eighty yards out and rowed the supplies out in a ship's boat. It was a laborious process; the dinghy had no rowlocks and Bobby had to improvise a pair with rope. Despite his wound and the danger of being fired on by both sides Bobby worked on and when the *Joan* was finally provisioned he took her under power to the junk. Two water barrels he found aboard were filled from four-gallon jerry cans.

After the supplies were stowed, it was the turn of the men. Rowley had called the battery together and told them of his plan to escape in the event of a surrender. He advised the married men and those whose pay was being made up by their civilian employers to stay. Their civilian pay, he explained, would end with their death and the chances of survival in the escape were not good. At least if they were prisoners their families would not suffer, he told them, and he advised them to join their sister battery on the other side of the airfield.

Rowley warned his gunners that, apart from the danger from the Japanese both by sea and from the air, there was also the risk of being fired on by their own coastal defence guns for disobeying the order to surrender. There were minefields, he told them, and he knew nothing of the sea to the south of the Island. At the end of the speech he waited. He had envisaged sharing the escapade with a small group of tough and determined soldiers but to his dismay all but a very few men volunteered to go with him. Although he realised their decision diminished the chances of success he knew he could not leave them behind.

The evacuation of the men began in a choppy sea with a strong tide running. Few of the men in Bobby's party could handle a boat so once again he faced the prospect of a long row. He shepherded the soldiers into the boat and began the back-breaking shuttle service, twelve men at a time to the *Joan*. Each trip took ten minutes out and ten minutes back and by the time the last man was safely aboard Bobby was exhausted. He climbed aboard the *Joan* and with a sigh lay on the bunk in her tiny cabin and immediately fell asleep.

Rowley's party, including Fraser, who had to reach the junk, were hammering planks on to half-finished dinghies to make them seaworthy. By this time he could hear the Japanese half a mile away across the airfield, and he knew there was little time left. He watched anxiously as one by one the boats in the ramshackle flotilla were launched. There were few oars and the men paddled with their steel helmets. Fraser, he noticed, left in some style in an unfinished motor cruiser, rowing to the junk with shortened planks.

Rowley watched the boats bobbing crazily and he wondered how many men would even complete this stage of their escape. It seemed as he watched them that the boats, some of them only half-built, must sink before they even reached the junk. But miraculously they stayed afloat and one by one the gunners were hoisted over the side.

At 8.30 p.m. the air-raid sirens started up for the last time, an all-clear lasting for at least five minutes. The official signal for the final surrender, thought Rowley bitterly; Willy Hargreaves had been right. Almost alone for a moment on the quayside Rowley looked about him. Sadly he remembered earlier visits to the yard. His own racing dinghy had been built there when he joined the Changi Yacht Club over two years ago. As he watched the city burning behind him he thought longingly of the days when there were parties and life held no greater problems than training his battery and winning the weekend dinghy races. He thought of the horses and the dog he had shot and the possessions he had been forced to leave behind in his house in Alexandra. All he now owned he carried in a small suitcase at his side.

The memory of the death of Kelso, the Border terrier, brought him back to the present and he looked down to see Yellow, his cocker spaniel. In the excitement of the past hours he had forgotten him. Now he thought of the journey ahead and how slim the chances were of making it successfully.

Reluctantly he grasped the dog's collar, stroked its head and slowly drew his pistol. Then he paused and straightened. He knew he could not kill Yellow. He called to a gunner who was watching him and handed over the dog and the revolver.

'Shoot him for me,' he said. It was more a plea than an order. The gunner nodded and took the dog away. There was a shot and the gunner came back and handed over the gun. Rowley scrambled into the last boat.

'Cast off,' he said.

3

ROWLEY'S BOARDING of the junk was less than graceful. After scrambling up a rope ladder in the dark he fell eight feet down into the hold, scraping the skin from his shins. Rubbing them ruefully, he looked about him. The junk was far larger than he had imagined and a giant tiller, festooned with pulleys and ropes, waved gently at the stern. He wondered how the average Chinese crew of six could ever have managed such a monster. Around him soldiers were sitting propped against the junk's side. He scrambled to his feet and made his way to the poop.

It was 2 am when the last man was safely embarked. The *Joan* held forty and there were at least 120 more on the *Conwy Castle*. On the poop Rowley and the other officers held a conference and Rowley decided to sail at once so as to be out of the harbour by daylight.

Bobby thought it was madness to try to get underway in the dark, surrounded as they were by other junks and with the minefields ahead of them. He said so with some force, but Rowley was determined and gave his sailing orders. Bobby shrugged and when the conference ended he rowed back to the *Joan* to resume his interrupted sleep whilst he waited for the junk to be made ready.

The *Conwy Castle* was 70 foot long and very wide in the beam. She had two masts and the tiller, 15 foot long, looked to the tired gunners like the trunk of a young tree. Among his officers Rowley had few who could handle a sailing craft. John Purvis, a dinghy sailor, who had been a fellow member of the Changi Yacht Club was one and Rowley ordered him to get men to pull at the two bow anchors swinging the bows of the junk so that it faced the open sea.

The black fibre anchor ropes felt coarse and heavy in the hands of the gunners who pulled at them and when they had finished Rowley ordered the anchors up. Only one anchor came and he reluctantly ordered the other cable to be cut. Luckily there was a wind from the north-east and slowly the great battened sails filled and the junk gathered way.

From the *Joan*, Bobby watched as the junk came sluggishly to life. He had ordered a rope to be passed to the *Conwy Castle*'s prow and starting his engine had tried to pull the cumbersome junk round to the south. But the *Joan* was less than half the size of the other boat and her engine lacked power. For a moment it looked to Bobby as though the escape would fail before it had begun and they would be stranded in the roads at the mercy of the first Japanese 'planes to spot them. Then the *Conwy Castle* slowly began to move and joyfully he cast off the tow rope. As the boats moved off the men looked back at the island. The reflected glow from the buildings on fire was trapped under the heavy black pall of fuel-oil smoke. In its light Rowley's attention was caught by a party in a small boat rowing towards the junk. They were shouting and at a range of 200 yards he could see that their weapons were pointing at his gunners.

He knew that an undisciplined party of armed strangers could bring his expedition to grief. He hailed them. 'If you try to board us we will fire.' To his relief, after shouts of abuse, the boat veered off and went on its own way.

When dawn broke the junk was sailing well, with Bobby in the *Joan* chugging along a little way off. They were temporarily safe, provided they could steer clear of the minefields. Rowley glanced anxiously at his sketchy chart in the growing light and peered out to sea. They had just cleared Blakang Mati and were off St John's Island when he realised that they were in a strong tide race and the water was shoaling. The tide was faster than the cumbersome junk could move. Rowley waited helplessly for the sounds which would tell him he was aground. They came soon enough and the sudden arrest of the junk's progress threw the officers on the poop off their feet. Rowley ran to the side and looked over into the sea. It was hopeless. They were firmly grounded on rock and sand. In his efforts to avoid the minefields Rowley had gone too far west and struck the sea bed in the shallow water.

Minutes later he was hailed from the *Joan*. After only two hours and with the Japanese pouring on to Singapore Island the escapers were trapped. They could almost hear the prison gates closing behind them.

After they had cast off Bobby had kept his engine at slow with the junk in view before him and to seaward. Before he went aground he had caught a glimpse of Peek Island silhouetted against the flames. When they struck bottom he realised that it made him a perfect target for any passing craft. With two other gunners he slipped over the side and for half an hour in the warm sea they floundered and pushed against the hull of the *Joan*. It was useless. Under the circumstances there seemed only one thing to do. Bobby led the gunners back on board and calmly settled down to sleep until the tide turned.

Hours later he was awakened by movement. It was now 6 am and the boat was rocking gently on the incoming tide. Once again Bobby and his gunners went overboard and this time their efforts were successful. With a final heave the *Joan* freed herself from the coral bed and bobbed freely on the tide. Bobby could see that the junk was still stuck fast and he ordered the *Joan* round to her aid, shouting for a line to pull the junk free.

Rowley felt the junk beginning to move under him and he thought she too was afloat. He had ordered an anchor out when they first went aground in an attempt at a kedge, but it was no use. If he risked raising the anchor in the strong tide the junk would be driven even further inshore and grounded beyond hope of re-floating.

Six times a rope was made fast but each time the tide beat the small engine and brought the *Joan* crashing into the side of the junk. The anchor line stayed taut but by now the launch and the kedge were no longer pulling together. Rowley could see only one possible end to the situation. He leaned over the side and waved to attract Bobby's attention.

'No use, old friend,' he called through cupped hands. 'I think it's about time you were pushing off.'

Bobby protested but Rowley was firm. 'Not much sense in us both hanging about. Make for Sumatra. South West. Its nearest shore is only about forty miles off. There's no point in us all being caught.'

Bobby wanted desperately to stay but he saw the sense of Rowley's command. 'I can take some more bodies,' he called.

Six of the gunners on the junk who said they could swim were ordered over to the *Joan*. They scrambled over the side and waded and swam towards the launch. One man was swept away by the tide race and was only saved at the last minute by a line from the *Joan*. The stranded gunners watched with envy as, her engine making white water under her stern, the launch made a last circle of the junk. They waved and settled down in low spirits to await their fate.

Daybreak brought the first Japanese planes. From the poop of the junk, Rowley waited for the attack that seemed inevitable. He had lost his military cap and was wearing a green felt hat that he had bought in Jermyn Street in 1936. It was old and battered but it had retained a jaunty style and he pulled it forward to cover his eyes from the rising sun which was blazing into his face.

The sun was neutral. It warmed the gunners who were packed into the hold sleeping or looking up at Rowley with a trust that made him uncomfortable. Its rays glanced off the silver skins of the Japanese aircraft in blades of bright light and in Singapore it warmed the backs if not the spirits of 60,000 prisoners, disconsolately awaiting the orders of their new masters.

As the day grew so the number of the aircraft increased. Bored in the anti-climax of the end of the campaign, the pilots swooped indiscriminately on the shipping in the Inner Harbour and its Outer Roads, closely examining those craft that roused their suspicions. Soon, Rowley knew, it would be the turn of the junk.

The poop in the stern of the craft was covered with an atap roof. It was sagging but provided some camouflage for the white limbs of the men beneath it. But the hold, where most of the gunners were crowded, was open to the skies and the light skins of the men was an obvious invitation to any air gunner whose plane flew low enough over its deck.

Rowley ordered the men in the hold to lie flat, covering their faces and arms and legs. B.S.M. Sharman stood over them with a handful of live ·303 ammunition, throwing rounds with painful accuracy, whenever an aircraft was near, at any soldier unwise enough to show a glimpse of white skin.

At his elbow Rowley heard a discreet cough. He turned to see Fraser at his side. It had somehow seemed natural for Fraser to join the officers and N.C.O.s on the poop and Rowley nodded a curt welcome.

'I think we've got visitors, sir,' he heard him say. Rowley walked quickly to the junk's side and looked in the direction of Peek Island, the nearest landfall. A rowing boat was bringing a group of Malays in the direction of the junk. Their bright sarongs seemed alien against the backcloth of war and Rowley watched them with some misgivings. A village that could lead the Japanese to virtually a complete battery with its N.C.O.s and officers could bring itself prosperity. Ruefully, Rowley conceded that it would be a rare native who could resist the lure.

The leader of the Malay party was standing in the prow of

the boat. He stood like a warrior but he kept a careful eye for the approach of aircraft. The even pull of the rowers made herring bones of broken water in the sea which had become calm and undisturbed by wavelets and when he came within calling distance, the Malay in the bows hailed the junk. Cursing his inability to speak in the man's language Rowley raised his green hat in what he hoped would be taken for a friendly greeting. He had a working knowledge of Army Urdu but he was hopeless in any of the dialects of Singapore and the islands which surrounded it.

Once again the discreet cough made its presence felt just south of his elbow. Rowley turned testily and saw that Fraser was once again by his side.

'Well, what is it?' he said shortly. 'I'm a bit busy at the moment.'

Fraser was apologetic.

'I don't want to shove my oar in, Sir, but if it's any help, I do speak Malay.' He waited.

Rowley looked at him in silence. In the days since Fraser had joined his battery there had been little opportunity to get to know him. Rowley had noticed with approval the speed with which Fraser picked up his new job and then turned to the solution of more immediate problems. Now he felt the glint of gold, pure gold.

'There's more to you, Fraser, than meets the eye.' He waved towards the junk bulkhead. 'Speak on. And for God's sake make it good. A lot may depend on it.'

Fraser nodded and loosed a torrent of fluent Malay that had Rowley blinking.

By this time the rowing boat had come up under the stern of the junk and a boatman was gripping the formidable rudder.

The man in the prow looked up at Fraser, shading his eyes from the sun as he listened intently to the unbroken flow of speech. Fraser stopped and beamed benevolently at the boatman. There were anxious moments and then the boatman's brown face broke into an answering grin. He waved his free hand gracefully and spoke briefly to Fraser, Fraser spoke again. The boatman answered. It seemed to Rowley that the two were set for a morning of animated conversation. He decided to take shares in the discreet cough department which until now Fraser had made his own. But he lacked the touch. Fraser turned quickly at the impatient bark which was the nearest to the original Rowley could manage.

'Sorry, sir. I was explaining our situation and the headman has been kind enough to invite us ashore. He says that we are welcome to take whatever boats we may need.'

'Fraser, this is not the Royal Yacht. We can dispense with formalities. Just let's get ashore.' Rowley turned to give brief orders to his other officers before clambering over the side to join Fraser who was already in the boat. After him came Sergeant Pearson, Lance Bombardier 'Paddy' Flanagan and a gunner.

Even on the short journey from the junk to the beach Rowley had time to feel relief. After a night stranded on the junk it was good to be moving through water again, whatever may be awaiting for them on the shore. Fraser explained that the boatman thought that even with such small boats as they could collect, it should be possible to refloat the junk at high tide. Rowley nodded his agreement and as they approached the island he noticed a number of rowing boats drawn up on the beach. Once in shallow water he eased himself over the side of the rowing boat and waded on to the sandy shore. On his shoulder he carried a Thompson sub-machine gun; a pistol and two grenades bumped at his side. On gaining the beach Rowley's first action was to clean his pistol with coconut oil; it had got wet in the landing. He had just finished and was testing the action when Fraser, who had disappeared with the Malays, rejoined him.

'There is a smallish motor boat and about twelve rowing boats,' he reported. 'Not really enough for our needs.'

Rowley took stock of their position. The junk provided the

only practical means of getting the men of his battery across the forty miles of sea which separated them from Sumatra. Although it was certain to fall eventually, the Dutch colony was for the time being safe and he felt that by now some sort of escape route might have been established. If only he could get the junk afloat and under way he and his battery had an even chance of crossing to Sumatra. From there they would have to play it by ear, either by sailing down the coast to Java or by crossing Sumatra and hoping for a passage across the Indian Ocean to Ceylon and safety.

He felt he was a sufficiently competent sailor to cross to Sumatra in a small boat but a junk was another matter. Fraser and some of the officers had sufficient resource for the journey. But the gunners who now lay in the hold of the junk were a different matter. Boarding the *Joan* in Singapore had shown that only a few gunners had any knowledge of seamanship and he remembered, too late, that they had all stayed on the *Joan*. The others were landsmen. Few could even swim. Leaving them was out of the question. The junk must be re-floated.

'Fraser,' he said, 'I'm going to take Pearson and the others to look around the islands for more motor boats. Either we can use them to refloat the junk or at the worst take off the men and island-hop to Sumatra. In the meantime I want you to go back to the junk. If I'm not back by high tide see what you can do about getting her off. If you succeed don't wait. Head after Bobby for Sumatra and with luck I'll join you there.'

It seemed to Fraser that Rowley was reducing his own chances. The islands could hold Japanese search parties and the chances of finding serviceable motor boats were slight. But he got to his feet and dusted the sand from his shorts.

'Very good, sir.' There was a pause. 'I do hope we meet again,' he added. Rowley smiled, 'So do I, Fraser. So do I.'

Fraser watched the others climb into the boat and set off

through the surf. He waved and then turned to make his way back to the junk.

Back on board the gunners were restless and uneasy. Water was rationed and the meagre provisions did not go far among a hundred men. They waited impatiently for the tide and their spirits rose with every new movement of the boat. At last Fraser judged that the time of high tide was nearing and he was glad when the Malay rowing boat was launched once more and came towards them.

'Can I help, tuan?' the boatman called. Fraser nodded gratefully and waited as the boat glided to the anchor rope and the men in her manhandled the heavy anchor inboard. They rowed some distance ahead of the junk until the rope was fully stretched and then dropped the anchor on to the sea bed. Fraser saw that their purpose was to kedge. It might just work.

He ordered the fittest and strongest of the gunners to lay hold of the anchor rope in the bow of the junk and to try to get the boat off the coral by pulling against the anchor, firmly embedded as it was in the sea bed. Neither the gunners nor the junior officers who remained seemed to think it odd that their newest recruit should have assumed command and they did as they were bid.

By now it was mid-day and the sun was at its height; sweat poured from the men's bodies as they strained at the ropes. But the junk was too firmly grounded and Fraser watched in anguish as the tide dropped once more leaving the heavy craft still firmly in the grip of the rocks.

For two days at each tide the men, by now almost totally exhausted, repeated the kedging drill. Betweentimes they spent long and frightening hours hiding under tarpaulins, ground sheets or any scraps of material they could find as the flights of Japanese 'planes over their heads became more frequent.

Each tide found the men and the Malay helpers weaker. Reluctantly Fraser realised that it would be impossible to refloat the junk without the help of powered craft so on the third day, as dawn was breaking, he decided to go ashore for a further conference with the fishermen.

The tide was low and the junk, high and dry on the rocks, was separated from the island by a fast flowing stretch of water about 200 yards wide. The Malays were either asleep in their huts or out of earshot of his calls so Fraser decided to swim ashore. He was a competent swimmer but the current was formidable and there was a strong likelihood that he would be swept out to sea and drowned. But the alternative was at best to be taken prisoner and at worst to be machine-gunned or blown to pieces in a bombing attack and Fraser decided to take his chance with the water. Lewis Davies, a subaltern in the battery offered to join him, although he admitted that he was a poor swimmer.

The two men stripped off their shirts and shoes which they draped around their necks and lowered themselves over the side of the junk. At first they waded in the clear water but it soon became too deep and they had to swim. Almost at once Fraser realised that the current was too strong for him; he was being swept away from the shore. Davies, when he saw that Fraser was in trouble, turned back and waded to the junk. In the centre of the channel was a navigational buoy and, as the current carried him past it, Fraser grabbed its chain and hung on until he had regained enough strength to climb on to it. From his uncertain perch he turned and waved to Davies. When he was rested he lowered himself into the water and swam slowly to the shore.

In the village he wakened one of the boatmen who agreed to fetch Davies; and while Fraser waited he tried to find out from the other Malays which islands were most likely to have boats with sufficient power to drag the junk back into the water. One of the fishermen said that on Pulau Blakang Padang there were many boats and he offered to take Fraser and Davies there in his sailing boat for a fee of 20 dollars. It was an absurdly high sum and Fraser had only 35 sodden dollars in the world. Davies, when he arrived, had none. But their need was so desperate that Fraser had no alternative but to accept. The Malay nodded and pocketed the money. Then he and another Malay led the two Europeans to a sailing boat in which they set off.

The Malay's greed had given Fraser an idea. 'It is a pity we were not on the junk,' he said. 'I could have paid you more.' He saw the Malay's eyes glint with interest and went on. 'The men have pooled their money as a prize for whoever refloats them. I believe they have about 300 dollars.'

It was true that the troops on the junk on Rowley's orders had pooled their resources and the sum amounted to 300 dollars. It seemed to Fraser that high though the price was, the men would gladly pay it to get on their way to freedom. He could tell by the way the Malay reacted—he was already planning with his companion to collect twenty more Malays and their boats—that the refloating was only a matter of time. He felt free to plan his own escape with Davies.

Blakang Padang was a dismal sight. The island beyond, Pulau Sambu, had been a naval re-fuelling halt and was a mass of huge, cylindrical oil tanks. They had been broached and their oil fired with the result that Blakang Padang was choked with a heavy black smoke like a winter fog.

Nor was the small native village where they landed attractive. All the huts were of corrugated iron, giving the place the look of a shanty town. The Malayan inhabitants were friendly enough but they told the two soldiers that the island's stocks of food were exhausted and that they had only coconuts to offer their guests.

That evening Fraser sought out the Penghulu, the village headman, and persuaded him to give them a supper of curry and tea. As they talked over their meal, stomachs full for the first time since the fall of Singapore, the headman warned them against a colony of Chinese who lived on the island. He told them that since the Japanese invasion the Chinese had looted and stolen from the Malay islanders.

'They are bad men, tuan,' he told Fraser. 'If they see you they will hand you over to your enemies. It is not safe for you to stay here. Tomorrow, at dawn, I will arrange for a boat that will take you to another island where you will be in less danger.'

Before lying down to sleep, Fraser and Davies arranged with the Penghulu to call them at six the next morning. But it was 7 am before he arrived and then the two, in a fever of impatience to be off, had to sit with him through the formalities of eating rice bread and drinking coffee. It seemed hours before at 8 am the Penghulu at last got to his feet and brushed the crumbs of rice bread from his sarong. He told Fraser that the boat they would take was through the jungle on the far coast of the island and motioned them to follow him down a path outside the hut. But he warned them that they must walk at least fifty yards behind him in case they were surprised by Japanese or caught by the Chinese looters.

'If it was known that I was helping you, I would be put to death and my village would be without a leader. In these times it is necessary that I should be here to help and advise the others. I hope you understand.'

* * *

In the days that followed, Fraser and Davies were to bless the friendly Malays who, at the risk of their own lives, ferried them from island to island on the route to Sumatra, fed them with fruit and coconuts and gave them coffee from their own inadequate stores. They were days of constant alarms. Time and again the boatmen whispered warnings as they spotted small craft crewed by Japanese passing near the boat. It was the signal for Fraser and Davies to crouch as low as they could get and wrap cloth round their heads to look like native crewmen.

Eventually they were brought to an island where they found two other British soldiers who had bought a motor boat from the natives. The men told Fraser that they planned to sail it to the mouth of the Indragiri river on the Sumatran coast and offered to take him and Davies with them. The soldiers showed Fraser a small compass and said they were going to head due west.

'We're bound to hit Sumatra,' said one with confidence. Fraser and Davies eagerly agreed.

For a day and a night they sailed across open sea and at dawn on the second day they saw the coast-line of Sumatra. As they neared it, a mile or so off shore they could see the lines of pagas, fishermen's bamboo huts built on stilts in the sea in which their owners sat with their lines and nets. At the first of them Fraser asked the occupant the direction of the Indragiri.

'Further south,' the fishermen called back. 'You must go further south.'

In this manner, stopping at pagas to ask directions the boat and its four occupants made their way down the coast. At one point they came near to grief when without warning the engine caught fire and threatened to ignite their stores of petrol. But Fraser peeled off his shirt and used it to smother the flames. Although he succeeded the shirt was ruined and he had to complete the journey with no covering for the upper part of his body.

At length the party came to the wide mouth of the Indragiri and turned the motor boat up-river. Progress was slow against the swift current but they persevered. For three days the only people they saw were Malays who paddled their boats along the edges of the river going about their normal daily routines. All the small villages were on the river's edge in jungle clearings and the water was their only highway. On the afternoon of the third day they saw they were approaching a large village. On the bank they could see a stoutly built quay with a road running by the river and a row of native shops along its length and as they came alongside they were heartened to see a crowd of Europeans. The village was Rengat, one of the Sumatran staging posts in a hastily-organized escape route across the island.

Thankfully Fraser's party tied up alongside a fairly large sea-going vessel and, as the four scrambled ashore, Fraser glanced idly at the name *Numbing* written in chipped and fading paint on her bows. But as he glanced up at the bridge his attention was suddenly riveted by a figure he saw sitting there studying a chart. Under a faded green hat he saw the familiar features of Rowley.

* * *

Rowley's arrival in Sumatra had been the result of a series of chances. After he left Fraser at the junk he and his N.C.O.s had been ferried round the maze of islands which make up the Rhiu Archipelago, looking for boats for the marooned soldiers on the *Conwy Castle*. He had found a small motor boat. As the victorious Japanese navy planes flew, at heights of 3,000 feet or more, over their craft, they carried out interminable reconnaissance patrols. None of them, Rowley noticed thankfully, seemed interested in his boat or the many small craft, some under power, others with pathetic scraps of sail which he saw during the day.

One day as they sailed with drooping spirits they saw amongst the islands one that seemed to have a larger community than others they had passed. Rowley swung his little boat towards a wooden quay and came up alongside. From above him a voice shouted, 'Hello, sir, nice of you to drop in.'

Rowley looked up and saw an artillery captain, Mike Pritchard, whom he had last seen in Singapore before war broke out. He climbed up the steps of the little quay, grinning. The two men chatted for a while when suddenly Rowley felt exhausted. In the warm evening sun his eyes began to smart and his tongue was dry. Mike's voice trailed away and Rowley realized with a shock that he was falling asleep on his feet. Apart from odd naps, he had not slept for four nights. He shook his head to recover his senses. 'Any boats round here?' he asked and Pritchard shook his head. 'No boats, no Malays, nothing. I'm not even sure where we are.'

Rowley felt in his technical haversack for the map he had taken from the child's bedroom in Singapore. Mike looked at it briefly. 'What's that island there?' he asked.

'India,' said Rowley. 'It's that sort of map.' He pointed to the other side of the paper, 'And that's Australia.'

'Great help,' commented Mike ironically. 'It may not have this island on it then?'

The past days had been frustrating. Time and again Rowley had been unable to tell whether he was sailing up an inlet or following a sea channel through a chain of islands. Hopes of finding more boats to collect his men which had been raised when he saw the wooden jetty were dashed as quickly as they had been raised. He lay on the boards of the quay and pulled his hat over his eyes. 'When in doubt—pass out,' he murmured. And just before sleep came he saw his N.C.O.s, one by one, following his example.

He woke before dawn the next morning. It had been an uncomfortable and cold night but the sleep had restored his resilience and he immediately began foraging for food and fuel. When his companions awoke they found him filling the tank of the motor boat. At his side he had collected a pile of coconuts.

'You'd better come with us, Mike,' he said. 'And I think we ought to make an early start. There's been quite a lot of Japanese air activity and I think the sooner we move on the better.'

For a long morning the motor boat cruised through chains of deserted islands and stretches of empty seas. By now Rowley was desperately worried about the fate of the men in the junk. He had been unable to find the boats he needed and every hour was putting him further and further away from their aid. At mid-day they saw an island with a cluster of atap-roofed houses on it. Malays in their sarongs walked under the palm trees. It looked so peaceful a scene to the men on the boat and so far removed from the horrors they had lived through.

Ashore they were given rice in the cups the Malay islanders used to collect the rubber they tapped from the trees. Gratefully Rowley accepted his and sank against the trunk of one of the bigger palms to eat it. There was suddenly a heavy rustle of palm leaves. A crashing thump, and the cup was smashed in Rowley's hands and he felt a quick stab of pain through his knee. In one movement he leapt to his feet, whirled round and his Thompson was at the ready, tucked between elbow and body. The Malays jumped for cover. Rowley relaxed when he saw his enemy. At the foot of the tree lay a huge coconut. His mind went back to the palms in which the Jap observers had nested and the stark trunks his guns had left.

He tried to cover his embarrassment with a joke. 'I think the trees are trying to get their own back,' he said. But at the thought of what would have happened if the coconut had struck his head a chill ran through him. It would have been hard to have come this far through the battle in safety only to have fallen on this peaceful little island with a fractured skull from a coconut. For the rest of the meal Rowley kept a respectful eye on the palm tree.

When they saw him put the gun down the Malays slowly began to return. The speed of his reaction had awed them and they vied with each other in advice for the white man and for the first time the men heard of the River Indragiri.

'There are many white soldiers, there,' a Malay assured them, 'and you will find friends and large boats to collect your men.'

Rowley had not planned to go as far as Sumatra to get help for his stranded battery, but the more he thought about it the more it seemed the only solution. Rather than use a flotilla of small boats to help refloat the junk he could see the advantage of a larger boat, powered and perhaps with a pilot, which could take off the gunners and bring them back to Sumatra at greater speed. He decided that the risk of going back into the Singapore roads which by now would be infested with Japanese patrols and shipping was justified and when he outlined his plan to the others they agreed to head for Sumatra.

That night the gunners slept on the boat. Although they were only a few miles from the Equator the nights were bitterly cold and Rowley slept fitfully. He was glad when the morning came and with it the warmth of the sun. After a shipboard meal of coconuts and rice, the boat's anchor was raised and the party set off more confidently for Sumatra. They had been cruising uneventfully for some hours when Rowley noticed that the water had changed from the brilliant green of the ocean to the sepia shades of a river. Without saying anything to his companions, he switched off the engine and felt the push of a current against the prow. He switched on the engine and said quietly,

'We've made it, we're here. We're in a river.'

The men in the boat stared at the sights which were coming up by them. On both banks mangrove trees made their gnarled progress to the water's edge. Before them, floating on a mat of green leaves, a blue cloud of water hyacinth spread fifty yards and more over the river's surface and bore down on the boat. Rowley and his companions were astonished by its beauty and watched hypnotized. It was only when the floating garden was within yards of the boat that they became alive to its danger. If the leaves and roots of the flowers choked the propeller the boat would be caught and they would be carried helplessly out to sea. With a sudden burst that sent his companions sprawling Rowley revved the boat's engine and swept in a wide white arc round the flowers which undulated over his wake, their blue heads nodding.

Later the unbroken acres of mangroves of the estuary gave way to palm trees and the land appeared to be getting firmer, the banks higher. They passed more beds of the hyacinth, more palm trees. Ships passed them, small but impressive-looking coasters with funnels and masts. They were just the sort he was looking for to collect the battery thought Rowley and changed course as a village came up over his bows. It was Rengat.

On the quay, waving to him to come alongside, was a portly figure wearing a General Service badge in his military cap. It was Major 'Jock' Campbell, a rubber planter before the war. A rugger and boxing blue, he had been sent, in the last days before the fall of Singapore, to help organize an escape route through Sumatra when it had become apparent that the Island's surrender was only a matter of time.

He helped Rowley ashore and took him along to meet the Dutch Controlleur, the senior civilian official in the port. Rowley was not slow in coming to the point. 'I want to borrow a boat,' he said. 'I've got some of my chaps still out there and I want to bring them in.'

The Controlleur was grave. 'There are many people in the islands out there,' he told Rowley. 'What of *them*? They have as much right to freedom as your men. Some are wounded and there are women too.'

Rowley eyed him shrewdly. 'You lend me a boat and I'll bring them in as well,' he offered.

The Dutchman smiled. 'Leave it with me. It is possible we may be able to do business,' he said. 'Go and wait on the quay-side for me.'

Rowley walked back to the quay with Jock in a fever of impatience. But a surprise awaited him that for a moment drove everything else out of his mind. Shy and smiling, a figure picked its way across the tangled ropes and hoses on the water's edge. It was Bobby Kennard.

The reunion was warm on both sides. In the days since they had parted Rowley had often wondered how Bobby was faring. The two men sat on a packing case and Bobby told him all that had happened.

Rowley discovered that Bobby had had neither map nor chart when they split up but he thought that a southerly course through the Dutch Islands would bring him to Sumatra and then he could follow the coast line until he found a sizeable village at which to land. On the *Joan* he had a 4″ compass which he put on the deck beside him and struck off accordingly.

The course the *Joan* set from Peek Island took her down a wide strait leading gradually and disconcertingly to the east. She passed a number of headlands and then it became clear that, to maintain direction, Bobby would have to choose at random a channel to go down. He turned south-east down a narrow strait and carried on until the sun told him that it was mid-day. Soon after, to his relief, they came to the open sea and later a small ship with a funnel hove into view. Bobby knew that in these waters the chances were that it was Japanese and for anxious moments he waited to be hailed. There was no shout from the ship and Bobby turned the *Joan*'s wheel to come alongside. His relief when a grinning white face appeared over the side was transparent and as the steamer slowed he caught the line which was thrown to him. The ship was the *Sir Hugh Fraser*—owned by the Singapore Water Transport Company. An Argyll officer, Ernest Gordon, had commandeered it at the fall to take off his men and was now steaming optimistically to freedom.

The two boats sailed in convoy until they sighted a native island where Gordon decided to put in for news and Bobby agreed to follow. It was a lucky landfall. A Gordon Highlander Captain named Ivan Lyon had formed there the first link in the Sumatra escape route. Lyon advised them to cross at night to avoid the danger of bombing attacks, so the *Joan* and the *Hugh Fraser* cast off at 7 pm to begin their dash across the sea.

Not excluding his time behind enemy lines on the Grik Road, it was the most uncomfortable night that Bobby had ever spent. The strain of following the *Sir Hugh* on a dark night at sea without lights was tremendous and after ten minutes Bobby was delighted to hand over the wheel to Gunner Spratley while he rested. The two men found that a thirty minute watch was as long as they could efficiently manage and spelled each other throughout the night.

Beyond the protection of the islands the open sea became choppy and the narrow and top-heavy *Joan* began to toss alarmingly. Worse, the movement loosened two large drums of diesel oil that had been lashed to the cabin roof and they began to roll dangerously, threatening to drag the *Joan* over.

It was a very relieved ship's company which watched the dawn climb leisurely out of the sea next day to show them a coastline ahead. They discovered that they had come too far south and the Joan followed the *Sir Hugh*'s wake as she turned and headed up the coast to the mouth of a wide river. They edged slowly up the river until at last they tied up at Rengat the day before Rowley himself arrived.

Rowley was entranced by Bobby's story. 'And what now?' he asked.

Said Bobby, 'I had a word with the boss man here before I met you. I gather from him that arrangements are in hand for transporting my party across to the West Coast where there is a better chance of a ship. We're waiting for some sort of transport now.'

'In fact,' he added, looking at his watch, 'I'd better be getting along to see what is happening. What about you?'

'Well,' said Rowley, 'I've still got the remains of a battery somewhere between here and Singapore. I think I should go back and look for them.'

'You won't come on with us, then?'

'Sorry, but I'd better go back. I'd be grateful if you would take my chaps with you, though. Mike Pritchard's with me and some N.C.O.s.'

'Of course I'll take them,' replied Bobby. He held out his hand.

'We always seem to be saying good-bye,' he said and there was sadness in his tone. Rowley shook the proferred hand.

'It won't always be like that, old man. You go on before, like John the Baptist. I'll probably catch you up.'

Bobby grinned: 'I wouldn't be surprised at that,' he said and walked away up to the village.

4

ROWLEY WATCHED Bobby limp away and wondered if he would ever see him again. He dismissed the thought and brought his mind back to the problem at hand. His anxiety for the men in his battery was mounting and it was with relief that he saw the Dutch Controlleur walking towards him. He was carrying a book in his hand and raised it in a wave as Rowley walked towards him.

The Dutchman's tone was brisk.

'You wanted a boat?' His English was broken, with a heavy Dutch accent.

'I do.'

'Then come with me.'

Rowley followed him to the edge of the jetty. As they walked the Controlleur explained that in the outer islands the British survivors of the many evacuee ships which had been sunk by the Japanese were stranded and helpless. If only they could be brought to Rengat they could be passed on through the escape route that had been set up on the island.

'No doubt among them are the soldiers of your battery. If I give you a boat, will you bring as many of them as you can to safety? It will give you a chance to help many of your countrymen and perhaps you will find your own soldiers.' Rowley agreed readily and the Controlleur pointed out to three boats moored in the river.

The first was a Naval landing craft. The Controlleur said, 'The landing craft is under the command of Lt-Commander Terry of your Navy and the ship next to it was once a Japanese fishing boat. She is the *Ko Fuku Maru*. Her Captain is an Australian called Reynolds. Between them they have already saved many lives.'

Rowley had already noticed the fishing boat. He had noticed, too, an attractive Chinese girl who was leaning over the ship's rail and thought that the girl looked in much better shape than the boat. The paintwork was chipped and dirty but Rowley thought that if it was one of the fishing boats the Japanese had used for espionage, as seemed likely, it would be equipped with the echo-sounding apparatus and other navigational aids which would be invaluable in his search for his battery back among the Thousand Islands.

But the Controlleur quickly dashed Rowley's hopes. 'The boat for you is the one lying next to her.'

He pointed to a 66-ton coastal launch with a short squat funnel, a bridge and two masts. Rowley was delighted. The *Numbing* was all that he could have hoped for. To be commissioned to such a large and workmanlike vessel was, for a land-bound gunner, nothing short of a bit of fun.

'What about navigation? Charts and so on?' he asked.

The Controlleur shrugged. 'Don't worry about that,' he said. 'There is a Malay pilot who knows the waters. He will come on board when you are ready to sail. But of course you will be the Captain.'

Rowley was finding difficulty in grasping his sudden translation from the army to the navy. It lacked the ceremonial that usually accompanied such an appointment. The Nelson touch was not apparent.

'What about a brief?' he asked. 'Ought I not to have some papers to show I have a right to take the ship?'

The Controlleur shook his head in disbelief at Rowley's formality.

'Things are very chaotic at the moment,' he said. 'I am

afraid that there are no proper channels for this sort of operation.'

But years in the army had taught Rowley that it was unwise to take over a large and expensive piece of equipment without a chit. He pressed for an authority. The Controlleur thought for a moment and then with another expressive shrug opened his book.

He asked, 'What is your name?' Rowley told him. On the fly-leaf of the book the Controlleur wrote the words: 'Major Rowley-Conwy is commissioned by the Royal Netherlands Government as Captain of the ship *Numbing* and should be allowed to proceed without let or hindrance.'

Solemnly he tore out the sheet and handed it to Rowley. Rowley accepted it gravely, folded it and tucked it into his technical haversack next to the map he had taken from the bedroom in Alexandra. Together the two men waited for the arrival of the Malay pilot. Rowley was eager to be off and he was delighted when coming round a bend in the river he caught sight of a rowing boat with a native sitting, rather grandly, in the stern sheets.

'Ah,' said the Dutch official his eyes lightening. 'The pilot. Good.' He slapped his book sharply against his thigh. 'You should be able to set off quite soon. That is good.'

Rowley eyed him in mild surprise. The Dutchman's change of manner puzzled him. But as the Malay climbed up the steps of the jetty the mystery was resolved. The Controlleur explained, 'You should perhaps know that he is not at all keen on going out in your ship.'

It was as massive an understatement as Rowley had yet heard. When the Malay neared the two men it was obvious that far from not being keen the Malay was violently opposed to the plan.

There is a point when emotion runs so high in a man that it leaps the barrier of language and the Malay made the jump effortlessly. The torrent he loosed when he reached them left Rowley with the uneasy feeling that his first duty as a skipper would almost certainly be the quelling of a mutiny. In an absent gesture he dropped his hand to the revolver holster on his hip. His intention was innocent but it merely served to confirm to the Malay the hazards into which the Controlleur was heartlessly hurling him. His eyes popped and for a moment Rowley thought he was going to leap into the river and disappear in the jungle on the far bank at a fast crawl.

Rowley hurriedly clasped his hands before him and bestowed what he hoped was a conciliatory smile on the luckless native. The native was unimpressed and it must be admitted that Rowley, in his torn khaki drill, his green hat pulled piratically over his eyes and a Thompson sub-machine gun slung over his shoulder, was not a sight calculated to soothe an agitated mind. The Malay turned to the Dutchman, arms waving. His eyes rolled, his uplifted palms quivered. But his appeal was wasted on the Dutchman who replied quickly, his tone forceful and firm. The Malay rapped his forehead with the heel of his hand and his fingers took off in a swallow dive of supplication. It was a formidable performance but the Dutchman was an unresponsive audience. His tone became yet more firm and whatever it was he said it had a telling effect on the pilot. At once the Malay shrugged and in sudden defeat made what was obviously a sullen agreement. Rowley wondered what threat could have been so powerful that it overrode the pilot's fear of the Japanese.

The Dutchman, now that victory had been won, spoke more softly to the Malay; then he turned to Rowley. 'And now,' he said, 'I think you will have no more trouble.'

Rowley doubted it. Catching the Malay's eyes was an uphill struggle but eventually he succeeded. He nodded and gestured to the *Numbing*. 'We go?' he said. The Malay's eyes went heavenwards in mute reproof at whichever local god had so basely deserted him and nodded. 'O-kay,' he replied, though plainly that was the last thing it was.

Rowley shook hands with the Dutchman and made off towards the rowing boat and with a last reproachful look at the Controlleur the Malay followed. The two men clambered into the boat and rowed out to the ship in a silence broken only by the oars in the water and the unfeeling mockery of a jungle bird's song in the trees on the opposite bank.

Aboard the *Numbing* it was Rowley's turn to be crestfallen when he saw the rations on which he was to live for the coming weeks. The shadowy depths of the hold were filled with rice sacks. But he brightened when he climbed down the companion way into the engine room and walked round the iron catwalk.

The engine was powerful and lovingly tended and its maker's name 'Deutz: Koln' shone from its plate. Whatever the short-comings of its pilot the *Numbing*'s engineer was a man in love with his job. For the first time since the pilot's arrival Rowley thought that there was a chance that good work could be done.

Back on deck Rowley mustered all hands. They were three. The pilot made no effort to hide his resentment, while a second man, whose oily hands showed him to be the engineer, was uncommunicative. The third member of the ship's company was a young native who made it clear that beyond casting off, tying up and tidying the ship, he was taking no responsibility for any part of the white man's foolishness.

Rowley continued his inspection of the *Numbing* followed by the scowling pilot. Just aft of the funnel he came upon a two-berth cabin and he slipped his technical haversack from his shoulder and dropped it on one of the bunks. He realised he was probably usurping the pilot's bunk, and that of the engineer too, but neither complained. Their major concern seemed to be to put as much of the ship as possible between them and himself. His base secure, Rowley turned his thoughts to the operation ahead of him. It was a daunting prospect. He was in command of a boat far larger than any he had ever handled, on a strange river and bound with a reluctant crew for unknown islands. 'In for a penny...' he thought optimistically and he gave the order to cast off.

The *Numbing* was tied up to a buoy. Rain up country had filled the river and turned the water the colour of chocolate. It churned muddily under the stern like milky cocoa as the ship's engines began to turn. With a deep sigh the Malay took the wheel and at once Rowley saw that whatever else was wrong the native's seamanship was beyond question. Getting the *Numbing* under way, turning her in the river and clearing the islands of water hyacinths which floated down past her was an operation which called for better than average skill. To counteract the pull of the heavy current it was necessary to start the boat at full throttle; but once she came athwart the tide the *Numbing* perversely shot off for the far bank. To counter this the pilot had to throttle down sharply and turn on full rudder with the current. Only then did the *Numbing* head quietly downstream.

When they came under way Rowley tried to read the river. As a boy fishing in North Wales his uncle, an admiral, had shown him that the deep water where the fish lay was always under the steep bank and never by the bank that sloped gently to the river. The Indragiri, while following the general principles of the Welsh streams, introduced variations that were quite its own. Often the steep bank alternated from side to side of the river with bewildering speed and Rowley could see that even the experienced Malay pilot was hard put to keep the *Numbing*'s keel from the shallows. But the pilot knew his river well and the *Numbing* sped downstream to the estuary making a good 12 knots. Rowley was forced to admire the way in which the pilot avoided the recurring trap of the water hyacinths but he wondered what would happen if they scraped the river bed at the alarming speed they were making.

Presently the river widened and the jungle receded and gave place to mangrove swamps which writhed and plunged their arthritic roots into the water. Rowley disliked the unhealthy-looking mangroves which sometimes stretched twelve feet or more out of the water. He asked for charts so that he could follow the boat's progress. Shamefacedly the

Malay produced a set which showed the waters round Palembang on the far south of the island. They were useless and those which would have shown the Indragiri estuary and the islands in which they were to sail were missing. Obviously the local charts had been appropriated by the pilot for the use of his friends. Rowley prayed that the Malay knew the river and its island-strewn estuary as well as his handling of the boat suggested.

That afternoon they saw the first Japanese aircraft. Within seconds the boat was heading determinedly for the nearest mangrove swamp and Rowley was all but thrown off his feet by the *Numbing*'s sudden turn. In his excitement the engineer forgot that he had an engine room telegraph and, head poking out of the engine room hatch, he chattered wildly at the helmsman. The aircraft was at least 12,000 feet high and, since Rowley had noticed vessels in rivers were left alone by the Japanese, he was puzzled at their alarm and the speed with which they were making for the shelter of the mangroves.

If they were going to shelter every time an enemy aircraft flew over at 12,000 feet they would never complete their journey. Rowley chafed impatiently until the plane disappeared and the pilot cautiously put the *Numbing*'s bow back into the middle river. It was hours before the mouth of the estuary and the blue open sea beyond came into view and, in the distance, the vague outlines of small islands. Before any preparations were made for the meal which Rowley and the Malays ate that night in a creek sheltered by mangroves, the Malays were careful to camouflage the *Numbing* with palm fronds and mangrove branches cut with parangs from the jungle. Consumed with impatience and hunger Rowley tried to explain that within the hour it would be pitch dark and camouflage would be unnecessary. But this fresh example of his recklessness found no favour with his crew. As they layered the superstructure with giant palm leaves they stole glances at their Captain and muttered in Malay amongst themselves. Though their views of white men who disregarded bombers and wanted to expose their boat to the fury of the Japanese Navy were mercifully lost on Rowley, their glances were eloquent.

At last supper was brought up to the bridge by the deck-hand and Rowley ate it hungrily. It consisted of rice and scraps of meat which he was unable to identify. But he had not eaten that day and he quickly cleared the little tin plate which had been offered to him.

The meal was scarcely over when from the river beyond their creek they heard the sound of oars. To the pilot this meant only one thing. The Japanese had landed in force and were seeking him out personally because he had aided the British. He ducked for cover under the palm fronds, followed by the engineer and the deck-hand, where, eyes rolling, they waited in silent apprehension.

The rowing boats which appeared came as an anti-climax. In the first boat sat a nurse and a huddled group of soldiers, their uniforms torn and muddy. Behind them were four more boats containing civilians, including two women. Although she was flying no flag the soldiers waved frantically when they saw the *Numbing* and under Rowley's orders the Malays helped them over the side. When they were safely aboard Rowley learned that they were survivors of an evacuee ship that had been bombed and sunk. With paddles and makeshift oars they had rowed more than twenty miles across the open sea from the island on which they had been beached. They were exhausted and weak with hunger.

The Malay deck-hand, unasked, brought cups filled with steaming rice and tins of condensed milk which he poured over the meal to give it flavour. Rowley nodded approvingly and the survivors grabbed at the bowls and ate hungrily. Then, their bowls empty, they fell asleep where they sat on the hard decks or on sacks of rice in the hold. Rowley had seldom seen human beings in such a state of exhaustion.

Lying on his bunk that night he reviewed the position. By

now they were out of the estuary and were surrounded by a mass of islands. His lack of communication with the pilot worried him for he noticed that the further from the river mouth the pilot went the more surly and uncommunicative he became. The survivors they had on board could give no very coherent account of what had happened and they were certainly too weak to help in the running of the ship. They had no idea where they were or where they had been. They told Rowley they had left Singapore as official evacuees on the evening of Friday the 13th. Soon their ship had been bombed and their fellow passengers killed in the raid or drowned later. Five rowing boats had been enough to hold all the survivors. They had reached an island and there they had lived on coconuts until they found the strength to continue their escape. Rowley knew what an unsatisfactory diet coconut was and he sympathised when they told him of the agonies of indigestion which had followed their meals. To them the *Numbing* was heaven-sent. They were on a modern well-found launch, the rowing was over and they were under the command of a British officer. The fact that the British officer was now wondering urgently what to do next was mercifully unknown to the sleepers who lay trustingly on the deck. Indeed, there seemed no immediate solution except to follow their example and soon Rowley too was fast alseep.

Although he awoke at first light, the Malays were ahead of him. From his bunk he could hear the first rumblings of the engine, and the smell of rice from the deck-hand's small stove wafted through the cabin hatchway. Rowley stretched, stood up and walked out on to the deck.

The pilot was scowling at the world but when Rowley emerged, his scowl became localised and it was obvious that his urgent wish was to get back to Rengat as quickly as the *Numbing* would carry him. But Rowley perversely ordered the anchor raised and the *Numbing* slid out of her anchorage heading further seawards. Rowley's battery was to the northeast but he remembered the Controlleur's mention of the wounded soldiers and civilians from the sunken transports who were stranded on the outer Islands; he decided that they must have priority and headed east.

The *Numbing* had not been steaming for long when a cry from the Malay deck-hand broke the morning quiet. Following the pointing finger Rowley saw what at first he thought was a school of basking porpoise. As they came nearer he saw the khaki and grey lumps were bodies of six or eight drowned soldiers. Swollen obscenely they sprawled on the surface of the water like great rag dolls, their shirt and trouser buttons burst under the force of their inflated bodies. He turned away, sickened. For a moment he contemplated firing into the bloated bodies in the hope that he could deflate them so that they could sink to some kind of peace on the ocean bed: but he did not want to alert the survivors they had picked up and he watched as they floated by, in helplessness.

Later they picked up more survivors in Malay fishing craft, made from the hollowed-out trunks of palm trees. Rowley was astonished that the soldiers had been able to manoeuvre these clumsy top-heavy craft across the choppy sea. When he took them aboard he learnt that some of the dug-outs had turned turtle the day before and the bodies which had floated by earlier may have been those of their occupants. The survivors' own boats were so perilously overcrowded that they had been unable to answer the pleas of help from their drowning companions.

The Malay pilot was still troubled by the reconnaissance planes and if cover was available in the shape of an island the *Numbing* made for it at a discreet half-speed so as not to show a white wake. Although worried by the possibility of attack from the air, Rowley had a theory that in a small boat with a good turn of speed it should be possible to watch bombs in the air and avoid them as they were falling and he alerted the engineer to give immediate full speed in the event of the aircraft showing any positive and unfriendly interest.

During the afternoon enemy air activity increased and the

Malay pilot was becoming visibly tense. At first Rowley dismissed the man's fears but the noise of a plane flying lower than the normal height for reconnaissance brought him sharply to the alert. With his glasses he picked out a fighter bomber at less than 5,000 feet. There was a deliberation in its flight towards them that raised the back hairs on Rowley's head. Though the nearest land was at least two or three miles away on the port hand, the distance did not deter the Malay. Sweat broke on his forehead as he headed for shelter and for once Rowley did not remonstrate. The purposeful approach of the plane was disquieting and he made no attempt to persuade the pilot to bring the *Numbing* back on to course. Behind him on the deck he could see the survivors he had collected lying exposed and vulnerable and he watched the plane alter course, bearing down on the *Numbing* on the port bow, crossing ahead of the craft. Rowley took up a position behind the pilot, hoping the steel sides of the bridge would protect him, and waited for the sound of the plane's machine guns.

Followed by every eye on the boat the plane circled slowly until it was set beyond the stern on the *Numbing*'s starboard quarter. An attack from the rear upset Rowley's calculations, his plans for evasive action called for a more sporting enemy. It was unfair to launch an attack from behind, he thought, as he watched a bomb door swing open underneath the plane.

The Malay pilot had seen enough. With an anguished yelp he abandoned the wheel in a frantic dive and scrambled down the deck for the comparative safety of the hold. In its sudden freedom the *Numbing* went into an uncontrolled turn to port and Rowley was sent spinning against the side of the bridge. Scrambling to his feet he darted back to the wheel and with one hand threw the little ship into a sharp starboard turn. At the half speed she was making in order to keep down the wake she was slow to answer to the helm and Rowley watched helplessly as two bombs detached themselves from their cradle. In a leisurely way they somersaulted into their flight path and bore down on the *Numbing*. He pushed the engine-room telegraph to full speed ahead but the reluctance with which the ship responded was paralysing. For what seemed a very long time the bombs dropped towards him as the *Numbing* sluggishly obeyed the command of the wheel. Then at last the rudder took a firmer grip of the water as the propeller began to turn faster, the ship started to heel and the *Numbing* came round to starboard. Even as they turned the shrill whistle of the bombs changed and two columns of white water broke the blue surface of the sea fifty yards to port, pillaring upwards. The ship shuddered with the concussion as the plane roared over the *Numbing* to bank in a wide circle to port for a return attack.

Already Rowley was getting the feel of the boat and he turned the *Numbing* to port to meet the bomber head on. As he watched, the plane completed a wide sweep and screamed in on a flat dive. Engine racing, the *Numbing* roared back her only challenge, speed and manoeuvrability. Rowley felt a wild elation. He had beaten the bomber once and he was determined to beat it a second time. Behind him, their timidness forgotten, the survivors watched, some terrified, some excited and shouting advice and encouragement.

Forcing himself to wait until the next flight of bombs had settled in their path he turned a shade to port then back to starboard and again to dead ahead. He was relieved to feel the *Numbing* answering with almost the nicety of a racing dinghy. Two bombs were falling to starboard and, warmed by a cheer from the survivors, Rowley turned to port, signalling to the engine room for yet more power.

Rowley could feel the sweat running down his back under his shirt. He turned at the wheel as the plane zoomed over to starboard at masthead height and waited to see what further tactic the Japs were to play.

But the bomber pilot had given him best. 'He's giving up,' a survivor shouted. 'He must have dropped all his bombs.'

It was true. As the occupants of the boat watched, the aircraft gained height. Soon it was a speck on the sky-line.

Settling his Jermyn Street hat more jauntily over his forehead, Rowley smiled broadly at the survivors who were by now hugging each other in delight and turned back to the wheel.

It was some minutes before first the hair and forehead and then, cautiously, the eyes of the Malay pilot appeared over the lip of the companionway. With slow precision he picked his way daintily through the sprawled legs of the soldiers, glancing uneasily over his shoulder in the direction in which the plane had disappeared. But by the time he arrived on the bridge he had recovered his self-possession and almost for the first time since they had left Rengat a wide grin split his face in half. Rowley smiled back and handed over the wheel. To approving nods from the Malay he settled on a bulkhead bench, drank a mug of water and thankfully lit a cigarette.

Moments later Rowley realised the reason for the pilot's sudden friendliness; the *Numbing* went into a 180-degree turn and headed determinedly back for Rengat. So far as the Malay was concerned enough was undoubtedly enough. Rowley threw his mug clattering on the deck and strode over to the wheel. He tapped the Malay angrily on the shoulder and stabbed his finger in the direction of the islands. The Malay shook his head frantically. Slowly with a meaningful look at the pilot Rowley unbuttoned the flap of his holster. It was the last straw. With a despairing cry the native once again released the wheel and scurried below. From the wheel-house Rowley could hear the frightened voice of the pilot and the deeper but equally angry tones of the engineer, but at least the *Numbing* was sailing in the right direction.

The deck-hand was the first man to emerge. To Rowley's surprise he was carrying a bowl of rice and a small spoon which he handed over with respectful ceremony. Rowley saw that the engineer was nodding and grinning from the engine-room hatch. Obviously there was a change of heart, at least so far as the engineer and the deck-hand were concerned.

For a while they sailed in a white swathe over a sea that

sparkled and shone. In time an island came up on the port beam and Rowley heard a burst of gunfire. He recognised the sound of a British bren and turned the wheel to port. Approaching the island, he saw through his binoculars a number of figures on the beach waving shirts and palm fronds.

Reluctantly the pilot came up to the bridge and took over. Free of the wheel, Rowley and the deck-hand dropped the ship's dinghy overboard and rowed towards the shore. For a moment as Rowley heard the *Numbing*'s engine ticking over behind him he was worried that the pilot might seize the chance to escape. He cursed himself for his stupidity in leaving the initiative in the Malay's hands and he was relieved when he saw the *Numbing*'s anchor splash into the surf.

On the beach an elderly European civilian ran to meet the dinghy. As Rowley waded ashore the European called out, 'There are about a hundred of us, soldiers, nurses and civilians. Our ship was bombed. Can you help us? We are down to the last of our food and water.'

As the survivors began to come down through the trees to the beach he was aghast at their numbers and wondered if he could take on so many. Certainly there were too many to be taken off in the dinghy. Rowley and the deck-hand waded out into the waves to direct the *Numbing* as near to the shore as they could safely bring her and to give an indication of the depth of the water. Then one by one they guided the people from the island through the surf to a rope ladder slung from the bow of the *Numbing*. Tended by nurses, survivors too badly wounded to wade were brought alongside in the dinghy and lifted in makeshift slings to safety.

That night they anchored in a mangrove swamp in the mouth of the Indragiri and from his bunk in the cabin Rowley heard the restless movements of the survivors and the occasional groans of the wounded. He was glad when the morning came and the *Numbing* weighed anchor.

5

THE MALAYS scrambled ashore as soon as the *Numbing* tied up at Rengat. Waving and grinning nervously they scurried up the quay and soon disappeared. There was little doubt that Rowley had seen the last of them and he wondered how he was going to manage without their help. He could not navigate and work the engines singlehanded, yet he saw no prospect of getting any of the villagers to assist him once the pilot had told them the story of his trip to the islands. His only hope, he knew, would be to find someone among the soldiers at Rengat who could sail a boat and work a biggish diesel.

He decided to go once more through the charts to see if any of them included the waters in which he was to sail and he was engrossed in a study of them when a hail from the quay broke his concentration. It was then, with relief, that he saw the grinning face and unruly shock of hair of Douglas Fraser. The two men exchanged stories until Rowley remembered his present problem.

'Know anything about engines?' he asked.

Fraser was unperturbed by the question. 'A bit,' he said. 'Why?'

'Think you can run this thing?'

Fraser looked round him curiously. 'She's a bit big and I've never done it before. Still, I'll have a go, sir. What's the drill?'

Rowley explained his hopes of finding the men from the battery. He was relieved when Fraser told him that by now, with the help of the Malays, the battery had almost certainly been refloated and their chances of coming upon the junk off the Sumatra coast were good. It was all the encouragement that Rowley needed and he was in a fever of impatience to be off down-river at once. Fraser restrained him with difficulty.

'I've no idea how the engines work, sir,' he protested. 'I'll have to get someone to show me before I can take them on.'

Rowley agreed and the two men decided to take their problem to Jock Campbell. He was an old friend of Douglas, who had worked on a Malay plantation with him before the war. It was Jock who had loaned Douglas a blue striped shirt when he arrived on Rengat naked to the waist.

Jock in turn soon found a Malay who, once he was sure that he wasn't going to be asked to sail in the *Numbing*, was willing to explain the workings of the engine.

Fraser had a mechanic's grasp and quickly absorbed the Malay's instructions. Soon he told Rowley, 'Shouldn't be much trouble, sir, as long as I can start her.'

It was less than reassuring. 'Start her?' said Rowley. 'Is it difficult?'

'If you don't get her going on the first four tries it's impossible,' Fraser rejoined brightly and beckoned Rowley to the engine room.

He explained how the diesel engine was started by bottles of compressed air which gave the pistons their initial impulsion. The bottles were usually recharged by a small auxiliary motor but the *Numbing* had none.

'What one has to do,' said Fraser, warming to his lecture, 'is to charge the bottles from the main engine. And, as there are only two bottles giving two tries each we have a four to one chance of being stranded whenever we shut down the engines. It's going to make things rather tricky.'

Rowley was inclined to be philosophical. With Fraser, a complete novice, in charge of the engine room and himself, equally raw, negotiating the hazardous course of the Indragiri it seemed unlikely that they would get far away before they ran aground.

'The problem may never arise,' he said and, with a brief nod, scrambled up the companionway to make his way to the bridge.

Fraser looked about the engine room. Like Rowley before him he was impressed by what he saw. Over the main engine block which was eight feet long and about five feet high a polished catwalk gleamed. There was a speaking tube for connection with the bridge and an engine-room telegraph dial for transmitting Rowley's orders to him.

The engine itself had two large dials. One was a rev counter, the other showed the state of the air pressure in the starting bottles. There were only two controls. One was a throttle which consisted of a small lever like the brake of a car and controlled the engine revolutions and the other a wheel to send the engine ahead or astern or, where necessary, shut it down altogether. Above the wheel was a pointer with a series of instructions. To the right, 'Start Ahead', then 'Run Ahead'. In the centre 'Stop' and to the left, 'Start Astern' and 'Run Astern'.

In happy anticipation Fraser beamed at the dial and waited for the signal to get under way whilst up on the bridge Rowley watched the rush of the current under his bow. He measured the 100 yards channel between the two banks, seeming suddenly so narrow, and reached for the engine-room telegraph.

Below in the engine room the telegraph clanged and the pointer on the dial went to slow ahead. Fraser turned the wheel to Start Ahead and waited anxiously for the explosive hiss of the air bottles. It came at last and was followed by more tense seconds until the engine slowly began to turn. At length he heard the thud of compression ignition and of the pistons settling into a steady rhythm and he turned the wheel gently to Run Ahead, adjusting the speed with the throttle.

As he translated the excited orders that were coming down the speaking tube he thought the whole thing was a good deal harder to accomplish than it had sounded when the engineer had explained it to him.

Meanwhile on the bridge Rowley was tied up in his own problems. He tried to remember exactly what the pilot had done but the fine detail had become obscured. The jetty of Rengat seemed to be coming up to meet the stern at an alarming rate. Alarmed, he swung the wheel, then throttled down sharply as the boat's bow was caught by current. Awkwardly the *Numbing* veered and then, to a long sigh from Rowley, settled in a course down river. Wiping his forehead with a forearm that was beaded with sweat, Rowley set his shoulders and settled to the wheel.

On the straight lengths of the river navigating the boat was merely a question of keeping in the middle where the water was deep and the current strongest. It was on the bends that difficulties arose. Mindful of the instructions of his uncle long ago Rowley hugged the steep bank but the contrary river shoaled so rapidly that they were in constant danger of grounding.

In the engine room a quiet harmony, man and machine, prevailed as Fraser hummed his way round his engine poking an oil can into its vital parts in what he hoped was a professional manner. But the atmosphere at the wheel was less relaxed and the varying pull of currents taxed Rowley's powers as a helmsman. It seemed to him that the *Numbing* was either rushing headlong at the current's pace or being involuntarily turned by a sudden contrary pull. Once or twice to his alarm the *Numbing* even seemed to check and to shudder as if touching bottom.

Rowley rang for more power and Fraser with a silent prayer had to push the engine beyond Full Ahead. The effect was startling. From the hatch of the engine room Fraser was dismayed to see a shower of sparks cascading out of the funnel. He called to Rowley, and Rowley, intent on the navigation, looked round testily.

'What is it?'

'Sparks,' replied his engineer. 'I'm just curious to know whether it's normal to get sparks out of the funnel of a diesel-engined vessel, sir.'

It was obvious that the question was not going to be answered and with an aggrieved shrug Fraser disappeared into the engine room again. Shortly the order came to decrease engine speed and a second glance at the funnel showed him smoke innocent of fire.

Soon the telegraph was ringing again and Fraser saw with amazement that the signal pointed to Full Astern. Since the *Numbing* had been going Full Ahead it was obviously an emergency.

His thoughts filled with pictures of collisions in mid-river, Fraser leapt for the controls. The drill, he knew, was first of all to stop engines then to restart them astern and slowly to increase revs. His hands flashing between the controls he carried out the difficult operation and then scrambled up the companionway to see what had happened.

An alarming sight greeted him. On a more than usually sharp bend in the river the *Numbing* had lost the deep water channel and was heading for the tangled jungle at the river's edge. As he watched there was a tremendous crash of breaking trees and the *Numbing* embedded her bows in the bank, branches and leaves cascading on to the bridge. A palm frond planed on the wind like a green gondola and floated gently past the aggrieved eyes of the skipper.

Fraser sought for the *mot juste* that would calm his superior officer.

'You will be glad to hear that sparks aren't coming from the funnel any more, sir,' he said and disappeared back into the engine room.

The *Numbing* was to run aground frequently during the first solo trip down the Indragiri and Douglas noticed that the water in the bilge was rising, despite the increased use of the pumps. The river was making exploratory inroads.

'Frankly, I don't think she'll stay afloat for another trip,' he warned Rowley. But Rowley's thoughts were still with the gunners he had left on the junk.

'Then we'll just have to get another boat,' he said and turned his attention back to the unruly river as the *Numbing*, leaking and groaning, ploughed on down stream past Tembilahan looking for survivors.

To the delight of the two men almost the first party they picked up were from the battery. B.S.M. Sharman and a number of Rowley's gunners, after a series of adventures had found themselves in a small boat at the mouth of the Indragiri. Although the junk had been refloated it had proved too difficult for the inexperienced gunners to handle and some had abandoned her in favour of smaller, easily handled boats. Sharman's party had by chance followed the same route as Rowley and were the first to reach Sumatra. Their delight at being hailed by their C.O. from the bridge of what looked to them to be almost a liner was boundless and, helped by Rowley and Douglas, they scrambled aboard the *Numbing* where they were immediately signed on as temporary crew.

It was with a much lighter heart that Rowley headed out into the estuary to search for the rest of his men. He found them in a bewildering array of craft and soon there were twenty or more gunners aboard.

Bit by bit the story of the *Conwy Castle* was pieced together. Purvis, who had stayed aboard, had managed with the help of the Malays enlisted by Douglas to refloat her and some of the gunners had elected to stay. The others, the ones Rowley was now collecting, had chosen to go on independently by smaller boats.

After another night near an unknown island, the *Numbing* was packed and the weight combined with the strain of towing a crowded fishing boat they had come upon was beginning to tell. Once again Douglas, whose legs by this time were badly swollen from the heat and diesel oil of the engine room, reported that she was taking on water alarmingly. Reluctantly, for he knew that there were many more boats in the estuary, Rowley decided to turn back to Tembilahan.

He had felt for a few hours the onset of a malaria attack and by the time the *Numbing* hove-to for the first night on the return journey, he was shivering uncontrollably. His head ached and the mangrove swamps swam before his eyes. He was worried about what would happen the next day if his malaria grew worse. Commanding the soldiers he had picked up was not easy. From many different units, they were armed and uneasy and discipline was difficult to enforce. They were reluctant to take orders from strange officers. Rowley wished he had another officer with whom he could share the responsibility of command and who, if his malaria did worsen, could take over until he was well again.

Suddenly the solution hit him with blinding clarity. If you can make a man a gunner, he thought, there is really no reason why you cannot promote him. Although until then the commissioning of officers had been largely the prerogative of King George VI, Rowley was never a man to hive off responsibility. He turned to B.S.M. Sharman who was with him on the bridge.

'Sergeant Major,' he said, 'I have decided to make Gunner Fraser an officer. Ask him to step up here, would you?'

The commissioning ceremony was brief and to the point. 'Douglas,' said Rowley, when Fraser joined him on the bridge, 'you've been doing a splendid job and I think it's time you had a spot of promotion.'

'Sir?'

'I'm going to make you an officer.'

'I see, sir.' There was a pause. 'Can you do that?'

'Frankly, I don't know, but I'm going to. After all there are plenty of precedents for commissioning men in the field and I suppose this could loosely be described as the field. In addition I am the senior officer present, so consider yourself commissioned. When we get to Rengat you'd better go and buy yourself some bits of black cloth and sew them on your shirt.'

He glanced at the blue and white civilian shirt that Fraser had borrowed from Jock Campbell. 'If nothing else, it will be colourful.'

As Rowley held out his hand Douglas noticed that it was shaking and recognised malaria symptoms.

'Why don't you go below, sir. I can look after things up here.'

The words fell happily on Rowley's ears. 'I think I'll do just that,' he said. 'Wake me in the morning.' And, scarcely knowing what he was doing, he made his way through the sleeping soldiers to the hold.

Once down he began feverishly to collect empty rice sacks and wrap them round his body for warmth. Then he wormed his way between the stores and waited for the bout to work itself off, alternately throwing off the sacks and wrapping them round again as burning heat and bitter cold swept over him in succession.

Afterwards he remembered little of the journey upstream. Incidents drifted together in his fever-gripped mind until eventually they tied up at the jetty at Rengat where he ushered the survivors off, cursing them in his fever for being slow and stupid. He was horribly tired and so drained that he had to lean against the bridge bulkhead for support. He hoped now that the greater part of the soldiers from his battery were safe but he decided that he would make one more trip, preferably in another boat, to the river mouth for a final search.

Then he would be free to plan his own escape.

* * *

There was no ceremony and no Controlleur. They saw a smaller craft that had come in to Rengat. And they took it.

The *Plover* was trimmer than the *Numbing* and easier to handle. Better still, there was an auxiliary petrol engine which charged the bottles of compressed air with which Douglas started the engines.

They had planned to take the *Plover* out into the estuary to search for more small boats but when they put in for fuel at Tembilahan they were ordered instead to take a complement of civilians and nurses back to Rengat. Survivors of bombed and sunk ships, the nurses, like Rowley and Douglas, were worn out. The two men watched in sympathy as the pathetic procession made its way up the gang-plank and the nurses settled down in the cramped and sparse accommodation on the deck and in the hold. It was pouring with rain in one of the worst of the 'Sumatras'—blinding thunderstorms which broke against the island's mountains—and the nurses were bedraggled and soaked. But they smiled as they reached for the warm rice Fraser passed among them.

The last nurse aboard and the *Plover* refuelled, Rowley cast off and turned the craft out into the river. She was low in the water and overloaded and she answered to the wheel sluggishly, but at least, Rowley thought, they were heading for home.

That night Douglas stood first watch and Rowley made for his cabin. It seemed he had hardly closed his eyes before he heard women's whispers at the door.

Said one, 'I can't go in there. The skipper's in there and he's in bed.'

'Don't take any notice of him,' the other replied, 'he's flat out. I've had two hours and he didn't even move.'

Half-asleep Rowley saw the figures of two of the nurses shadowed in the doorway. As he watched the girl who had spoken first tip-toed into the cabin and sat on the edge of the empty bunk beside him. He heard in growing dismay the nurse kick off her shoes and unfasten her belt and blouse. He waited no longer. Shutting his eyes firmly, he turned to the wall and went to sleep.

He was woken by the return of Douglas. It was getting light and he realised with a shock that the nurse was still in the opposite bunk. She awoke at Douglas' entry, her eyes wide and with a yelp reached for her blouse and fled from the cabin. Rowley waited in embarrassment for the inquiring look, the knowing gesture. But he had underestimated his companion. True to the code of the gentleman, Douglas betrayed no surprise nor gave a hint of his thoughts.

'Sorry to disturb you,' said Douglas imperturbably. 'Fairly quiet sort of night.'

6

THE 'TOURIST ROUTE' was a life line that stretched from Tembilahan, near the mouth of the Indragiri, across the island of Sumatra to Padang where boats took the Singapore escapees to India and freedom. It had been set up secretly before Malaya fell by a small group of men, some of them civilians, who mapped out an escape road which had its clearing house at Rengat. From there the escapers were taken 250 miles by truck and train across the island to Padang, a west coast port, and at points along the journey were helped by various Dutch, Malays and Chinese. It was a triumph of organization which could adapt itself to almost any change of circumstance and drew its executive personnel from the men who were using its facilities. Rank had no privilege on the route. Escapees were passed along it in the order of their arrival at Rengat. Colonels, even Governors Designate, waited their turn with private soldiers and civilian clerks.

The escape route worked perfectly and when on 8 March the Dutch East Indies surrendered to the Japanese only 800 Allied men and women were left on the island.

Characteristically Rowley had decided not to use the orthodox route. As the *Plover* came alongside the wooden jetty for the last time he reached for the engine-room telegraph and rang Stop. Within a few minutes Fraser, wiping his hands on an oily rag, joined him on the bridge.

'That's it, Douglas,' Rowley told him. 'If any more people come I'm afraid they're going to have to make their own way up the river.'

Douglas nodded and made his way to the bow to throw a rope to a waiting Malay. Rowley joined him and the two men walked down the gang-plank in search of Jock Campbell.

The other skippers had already made their plans. Bill Reynolds had announced his intention of sailing the *Maru* up the Malacca Straits between Malaya and Sumatra across the Indian Ocean first to Ceylon and then, if the fishing boat could make it, to Bombay. Rowley had considered his plan and at first thought of following him in the *Plover*. He even went to the lengths of taking on extra diesel oil in preparation for the trip. But in the event he decided that the chances of success were slim and abandoned the idea. The *Ko Fuku Maru* was only 78 feet long with a beam of 10 ft 6 inches. Her engine was held together with copper wire and her wheelhouse was only six feet square. The wheelhouse had a half-glassed front and sides and contained, besides the wooden wheel, an old binnacle and a standard compass. There was a bunk down one side of the house with a chart table that had to be folded into the ceiling. The galley was aft and consisted of little more than canvas curtains surrounding an oil stove. The ship's lavatory was a hole punched into the deck, Japanese style, and the ramshackle engine was below the stern. Yet Reynolds with a load of Chinese refugees sailed her successfully over 2,000 miles to India.

The more he thought of it the more Padang seemed to Rowley the logical destination and he discussed with Jock how he and Douglas should get there. The *Plover* was too big to take them further up-river and Jock suggested they should try to take one of the small log-burning steam-driven vessels that plied between Rengat and the villages up-country. Rowley was uncertain. The log-burners were 30-foot long, low freeboard boats powered by an Emmett-like steam engine. However, there was nothing else available and they arranged with a Malay crew to join their boat in the morning.

The two slept that night on the *Plover* and in the morning Rowley went to a quayside shop and bought two new jersey-knit fawn shirts. His kit now consisted of one pair of shoes, two pairs of stockings, one pair of khaki shorts, a dirty military shirt which he had worn since he left Singapore three weeks earlier, the Jermyn Street hat, a pistol and a Thompson sub-machine gun. Douglas was in even worse straits. He possessed only the shirt that Jock had loaned him and the shorts he wore. His shoes were disintegrating on his feet, rotted by the diesel oil from the *Plover*'s engine room.

Everything he saw of the log-burner increased Rowley's misgivings. So far as he could see the pile of logs that was her fuel was not enough to take them any distance up-river when he wondered what would happen when the wood was used up. His misgivings increased when at length the launch moved out into the river. It seemed to him that the Malays were putting on wood at an extravagant rate. But he remembered that for the first time in many days he was a passenger and the responsibility for arrival belonged to someone else. It was a happy thought.

For days he had been making decisions for himself and the hundreds of survivors he had rescued, decisions that could have made the difference between life and death for the people who depended on him. It was a pleasant change to sit in the shade of the little awning and let someone else do the worrying. His spirits lightened and it was a tranquil Rowley who watched the banks of the Indragiri slip past in the wake of the boat. Even his worries about fuel proved groundless. At intervals on the bank there were neat stacks of logs sawn and piled and as the boat's fuel got low so it was replenished by the Malay crew. Rowley smiled at Douglas.

'A very neat and well-thought-out little operation,' he

observed approvingly. 'Very encouraging. I rather think we are going to be all right.'

Douglas was dozing quietly and did not answer, so Rowley turned his attention to his fellow passengers, a party of sailors and thirty ragged soldiers. They sat, for the most part, in silence like tube travellers. Now and again a soldier would attempt a joke but the smiles it brought were tired and uneasy. They had lived through too much horror in the days since Singapore had fallen and in all of them Rowley sensed the trepidation of men who waited, dully, for the worst.

His was not a nature which would admit despair. He realized that it was only by a series of the most incredibly lucky chances that he had been able to get as far as Sumatra and secure his place on this curious vessel. Where Rowley differed from the men around him was that he saw no reason why his good fortune should not continue. The possibility of falling at last into Japanese hands he dismissed as defeatism of the worst sort. And yet it was a possibility and a strong one. The Japanese had landed at Palembang on the southeast coast of Sumatra on 15 February and only 270 miles of thinly defended country separated them from Rengat. As more Japanese landed at Medan and on other parts of the north of the island and marched to meet the battalions which had landed at Palembang, Rowley's party were in growing danger of being sandwiched between their two fronts.

When at last the launch tied up for the night, Rowley was amongst the first ashore, leading the party of sailors and ready for the next challenge in the escape. He was dismayed to discover that he had landed at the rubber factory which was the second stage of the official escape route. Long huts surrounded a bungalow that in peace time had housed the European manager. Now it was the headquarters of a camp staff and in the wooden huts soldiers of every kind were billeted waiting for their turn to be transported to safety.

The sight of a man in a green hat followed by another in a blue and white striped shirt leading a party of seamen produced a flicker of interest even amongst the exhausted British and Indian soldiers who were slumped against the walls of huts or standing in small restless groups at the edge of the rubber trees. But Rowley and Douglas were too engrossed in the thought of food to care about the stares. The semaphore smells of boiling rice had signalled to them and Rowley answered willingly. Fortunately the cook-house was not hard to find, and though the taste of rice was rapidly losing favour with him they were starving.

Whatever the limitations of the diet there was no shortage of eating utensils. When the camp was set up the organizers had discovered a store of the glazed white cups that were used to catch the rubber as it was drained from the tree. Rowley took one from the pile by the cook-house and watched as a cook filled it with rice. He lifted his broken spoon, the souvenir of the first trip in the *Numbing*, and tilted it, letting the rice fall in a watery stream back into the cup. His face screwed in distaste, he swallowed the bowl's contents. He waited for Douglas to finish, then got to his feet.

'Come on,' he said. 'We'd better make our number with the C.O., whoever he is.'

Rowley was uneasy. His plan for crossing Sumatra had been to keep away from the approved military routes which he knew could only slow down his party and he was dismayed to find that the rubber factory contained at least 500 men and women. On the 'first come—first served' principle he could be there for months.

At the bungalow they were shown into the office of the Camp Commandant. Lt-Colonel F. J. Dillon had been on the staff of the 18th Division which had arrived in Singapore only two or three weeks before the surrender. He had left Singapore as an official evacuee on Friday, February 13th, and he had worked his way to the rubber factory where now he was trying to bring some order into the administration of the camp.

Introductions completed and a very severe glare sent on its

way from the Colonel to the green felt hat, Rowley thought it high time to bring the meeting to order.

'Well, sir,' he said pleasantly, 'thanks for the meal. We won't get in your way any longer. We'll be off in the morning.'

The sleepless nights of the escape and the worries of running the camp had combined to shorten the colonel's temper to a high flash point.

'You'll do nothing of the kind,' he retorted. 'This is a properly organized escape route and we work on a first in, first out, basis. So will you.'

In vain Rowley tried to point out he was not an official evacuee but an escaped POW and that his plan had always been to take his small party on from Rengat by his own efforts; he had only come to the rubber factory because the log-burner had tied up at her jetty. But the Colonel was obdurate.

'There is an organization here and as long as I am responsible for it regulations will be maintained. You will wait in the camp until you are instructed to move on and that is all I have to say to you. You may go.'

Rowley saluted and walked away from the bungalow followed by a disconsolate Douglas. When they were out of earshot Douglas caught up and said, 'That's torn it. We could be here for days.'

Rowley turned with an impish grin, 'Think so? I don't remember seeing anything in King's Regulations about escaping by numbers.'

He paused. 'The sailors can come or stay as they wish, but you and I are off like lamplighters the first chance we get.'

It was still dark when Rowley wakened that night on the floor of one of the long wooden sheds which before the war had been quarters for the estate coolies. He listened for a moment to the night noises, the heavy breathing and the snores and the occasional cry of a dreamer living again an earlier terror, mingled with the ever present sounds of the jungle. Leading a party of men through the jungle at night seemed in the noisy dark a daunting undertaking. Firstly on the junk, then on the small boats and now in Sumatra he had shouldered responsibilities for other people. In the drowsy content of waking he wished he could just wait in comfort for a car to draw up at the door of the hut and drive him to Padang and a berth in a P. and O. liner.

'Blimey, what a hope,' he thought and forced himself back to reality. He wakened Douglas who was sleeping next to him and he in turn collected the sailors who were all eager to join the escape. They made their way out of the hut and collected in a loose group on the dirt road outside. Rowley put a finger to his lips and led them to the outskirts of the factory where a wider dust road stretched before them.

It was pleasant walking in the night on a road that did not meander but unfolded in a straight line between the battalions of rubber trees in their orderly ranks. Behind him he could hear the reassuring crunch of the boots of the naval party and at his side Douglas was striding out happily. Soon it was fully light and after they had been marching for about two hours a new sound, unmistakably a heavy vehicle, joined the other jungle noises about them. There was no need to give an order. As one the party left the road and leapt for cover. At best, Rowley thought, their defection had been discovered at the camp and the lorry was coming to bring them back to the factory and an unpleasant few minutes with an irate Colonel Dillon. At worst it could be a Japanese troop convoy.

But the lorry that came into sight in the growing light was plainly not a military vehicle. Rowley and Douglas, followed by the sailors, ran out into the road waving and the Malay driver brought the lorry to a halt.

'Want a lift?' he asked.

'Please,' said Rowley, scrambling up into the cab and waving the others to climb aboard.

'Where are you going?' he asked.

'To Bashra,' the Malay grinned. 'You will be all right there. The Emir will help.'

The Emir of Bashra, thought Rowley. It had an Arabian Nights ring to it and he had a picture of minarets and houris and smoking bubble pipes by the side of sparkling fountains. But he knew that the Emir's kingdom was more likely to be a small collection of down-at-heel atap-roofed huts and yet more rice.

In the event he was proved right. It was a nondescript village built round a market place which was bounded by rough wooden benches. It was mid-day and a good-looking young Malay in a gay sarong was waiting for the truck. 'The Emir,' explained the driver as he brought the lorry to a halt.

When the Emir saw the British party jump down from the truck he advanced towards them smiling courteously, his hands outstretched in welcome.

His English was faultless. 'On your way home?' he asked.

Rowley smiled at the words. 'Hope so,' he replied.

'Good,' said the Emir. 'Come, let us eat.'

He led the way to a hut larger and neater than the rest, where a pretty Malay girl was waiting. The Emir spoke to her and she began to prepare a meal. Inevitably it was rice but Rowley noticed with delight the dark stain of a meat sauce and the party ate hungrily and in silence.

The Emir waited until they had finished and then took them out on to the verandah. He listened as Rowley outlined the party's plan to get to Padang to board a ship to Ceylon.

'You have many miles to go,' he told them. 'From here you must go to Sawahloento which is in the mountains. It is a stiff climb, I am afraid, and it may be that it is too much for you.'

He thought for a while as the white men waited.

'I think it would be better if you stayed with us today and tonight. Tomorrow a truck will go from this village to Sawahloento and I will speak to the driver. He will take you with him but I fear that is as much help as we dare give you.

We do not know how near the Japanese are by now and I must think of the people of my village.'

Rowley understood the Emir's position and sympathized with him. If it were discovered by the advancing Japs that he had given any more than compulsory assistance to the retreating British his life and that of the people of his village would be at risk. He offered to leave at once but the Emir shook his head.

'You will be quite safe until the morning. And now I suggest that you get as much rest as you can during the next twenty-four hours so that you will be fresh to continue your journey.'

Rowley agreed and after thanking the Emir for his hospitality, led his party out into the village. When at length night came, it was obvious the Emir was torn between his natural sense of hospitality and the need to protect his family from future harm at Japanese hands. He wanted to offer the party places in his home but the future dangers worried him. Rowley sensed his dilemma and after conferring with Douglas, put the Emir at rest.

'We would not dream of intruding on you any more,' he said. 'We will be quite comfortable here on the benches in the market place and handy for the lorry in the morning.'

It was one of the most uncomfortable nights the party had ever spent. The benches became festive boards round which, it seemed, every mosquito in Sumatra gathered to dine. In agony the men slapped and slaughtered but the mosquitoes who died were replaced by other, hungrier insects. Rowley cursed and slapped. He pulled his stockings over his knees but the voracious mosquitoes pushed the strands of wool aside and bit into the skin beneath. In vain he buttoned his net shirt to the neck and pulled his hat over his ears. When morning did come after a night of little sleep the bodies of the whole party were swollen like pumpkins. Climbing up into the rickety lorry was agony.

Fortunately the breeze that built up when the lorry moved

off soothed their irritated skins and by degrees they began to feel better. Then, too, they were climbing into mountains not unlike those that Rowley had known at home in North Wales and he welcomed the cool mountain air. The lorry was less in sympathy with mountains. Its gears ground and the whine of its elderly engine became more pronounced the higher they climbed, but, coaxed by the driver, as the sun set it brought them, steam pouring from the bonnet, to Sawahloento.

It was a good arrival. The journey had taken them most of the day and the painful bites of the mosquitoes had subsided. In the growing darkness Rowley saw with approval stone houses, the first he had seen for many days, and he thanked the driver and jumped down. To his alarm he discovered that he had arrived at another of the army's escape route staging posts. Time was getting short and he didn't want to find himself at the back of yet another long queue with the Japanese breathing down the necks of his party. Happily, the organization at this small clearing point was concerned only with the broadest principles of escape. His party were fed and shown the village hall where they were to sleep. Once again there were no beds but there were far fewer evacuees than at the rubber factory.

The floor was hard but the hall was comparatively free of mosquitoes. As his party settled around him Rowley humped his two shirts and a towel into his technical haversack and, making a small pillow, settled down to sleep.

It was then that he heard the noise. Alien but unmistakable it floated into the hall. Rowley sat bolt upright in disbelief. It was a train whistle. Sawahloento was a rail-head. Their worries were at an end. Whatever was in store for them at Padang at least they would arrive there in the comfort of a train. Rowley slid into a deep and contented sleep.

It was a light-hearted party which hurried next morning to the railway station. No one attempted to stop them and they were told that a train for Padang would leave within the hour.

The party reminded Douglas irresistibly of childhood outings to the seaside and when the train arrived he swung up into the carriage with delight. The reassuring movement of the train rocked Rowley, his head fell forward and the talk of the rest of the party became a confused scramble of words which eventually died in silence. He dropped gratefully into a dark empty valley of unconsciousness. It seemed only a moment later when he was awakened by Douglas shaking his shoulder. The voice came faintly and then stronger as he came back to life.

'Wake up, sir. We're here. It's Padang.'

7

PADANG WAS crowded with soldiers and civilians. When Rowley's party arrived on 5 March, they learned that the last two large ships in which it was planned to evacuate survivors were on the point of leaving and that all accommodation was filled. Unless they could find a smaller boat in which to escape they were trapped and lost.

Sadly Rowley took his party to the Netherlands Hotel. Here he was able to get news of Bobby Kennard and the twenty gunners from the battery who were with him. He learned that Bobby had arrived in Padang some days earlier and had been billeted in a school nearby. Bobby and his party of gunners had embarked across the Bay of Bengal in an unarmed and unaccompanied 1,200-ton cargo boat which took off 36 officers and 66 men. Because of his wound Bobby was given one of the seven bunks available but the other officers slept on the foredeck and the men between decks under awnings.

Rowley was alarmed to learn that the boat on which his old friend had sailed was carrying a cargo of 900 tons of bombs. The captain's only navigational aid was a school atlas and there were provisions for only 3½ days on a voyage which took ten days to complete. But with Bobby as messing officer and two sappers supervising the native cooks the rice, the 96 tins of herring and the 21 lbs of bully beef which comprised their stores, lasted until they reached Colombo Harbour and safety.

*　*　*

By the time Rowley and his party arrived at Padang there were more than 2,000 Australians, Indians and British personnel, some of them deserters, in the town and it was alive with rumours of Jap advances.

Colonel Warren, a member of an Anglo-Irish family and a Royal Marine regular officer was in overall command. He had been the boldest member of the Special Operations Executive during the Malayan campaign. He had organized bands of irregulars and led raiding parties of great daring behind the lines and now he was trying to extricate the last of the trapped soldiers from under the noses of the enemy.

Colonel Warren had his headquarters in the Oranje hotel and in the evening Rowley and Douglas made a point of dining there to try to pick up any news of small ships for their own escape. In an earlier interview Warren had warned Rowley of the consequences that would follow if he tried to steal a boat. The Dutch, as the war news became worse, were becoming increasingly touchy in their relationship with the British but the warning was unnecessary. Rowley had already noticed that wherever he went, a discreet civilian followed him and he confined himself to trying to buy the vessel he needed. But the demand was so great that the price of any craft that would float was astronomic, far beyond the resources of his little party whose only capital was a small stock of Dutch guilders which Rowley had changed for the 200 dollars he had brought from Singapore.

One evening as Rowley, Douglas and Lt Lewis Davies, whom they had met in the city, were dining quietly they noticed at a table nearby the Dutch Commandant's adjutant and his wife, whom Rowley knew slightly. As they watched a soldier hurried over to the adjutant and whispered something to him. The Dutch officer got up and went to the telephone and Rowley watched him return looking grave and shaken. He said a few words to his wife who put her head in her hands and bowed over the table.

'Douglas,' said Rowley, 'Java has fallen.'

The next day was alive with rumour and Rowley was relieved when at 4 pm Colonel Warren sent for him.

Warren's note said that he wanted to see the gunner alone. Mystified, Rowley presented himself at Warren's office and the older man answered his salute. Without formality he began, 'I have arranged a sailing boat to take certain key personnel to Colombo. There is room for you and one of your officers. I want to know about them both.'

Rowley thought quickly and then gave a brief run down on Fraser and Davies.

'Which will you take?' asked Warren.

Rowley hated the thought of having to choose safety for one and almost inevitable capture for the other but he tried to view the two men dispassionately. In the end he settled for the one he knew best.

'Fraser,' he said and he was relieved when Warren replied, 'Yes, I agree with you. Go back and alert him but say nothing to anybody but him. You can take no kit except one haversack.'

Rowley grinned, 'That's no worry, sir. We haven't got anything else.'

Back at the hotel Rowley faced an unhappy job reluctantly. He knew that he had to make some explanation to Lewis Davies. In the end he told him that he and Fraser had been selected for a suicide mission. He excused the fiction to himself with the reflection that the chances against their surviving were slight.

He said, 'You must stay with Colonel Warren.'

Years later Rowley could still see Davies' face when he realised he was being left but he was never to discover what happened to the young subaltern.

It was dark when Colonel Warren next sent for Rowley

and Douglas. The rendezvous was a large, well-appointed and airy Dutch Colonial house on the outskirts of the town. It was raining hard and when the two men arrived they found a group of army officers already on the verandah. A moment later Colonel Warren stepped out of the house to join them.

As Warren spoke the rain drummed on the atap of the verandah roof. One by one he went through the line of people in front of him explaining why each had been chosen. Amongst the men Rowley recognised Jock Campbell and Ivan Lyon, the captain in the Gordon Highlanders he had met at Tembilahan. A senior Malayan civil servant named Broome, whom he was later to learn had been with Warren in S.O.E., was appointed leader. The party also included an artillery major, Bill Waller and Captain Clavel Spanton of the Manchester Regiment, who had escaped from Singapore together in a rowing boat and had been one of a party picked up by Rowley at the river mouth, 'Tojo' Clark, a Japanese military interpreter, a Police Superintendent named Davis and 'Doc' Davies, a Dermatologist in Malayan Command. Six Naval officers, a Chinese and a Malayan joined the party later.

As the Colonel spoke to each man in turn a movement in the dark and the rain beyond the verandah caught Rowley's eye. He peered out to see a line of tongahs drawn up outside the house. A tongah is a high wheeled pony trap and when Warren had finished speaking the men followed him to the verandah's edge where he motioned them into the waiting carts. Rowley was the last in line and as he passed, Warren laid a restraining hand on his arm.

'You're a very lucky young man,' he said. 'I had intended to make you Commandant of the British troops in Padang and go myself on this trip. Luckily for you, you're far too young so you get the trip and I stay.'

Nodding his thanks, Rowley climbed into the last tongah where Douglas was waiting. Then as the men listened, rain streaming down his face, Warren stood at the head of the little line of carts and spoke again.

He told them, 'Seven miles up the coast you will find a fully equipped Malay prahu. You will board her and proceed to Ceylon.'

It was a short enough briefing, Rowley thought, for a 1,500 mile journey across the Indian Ocean during the monsoon season. And as he followed the first of the line of tongahs whose little oil lamps bobbed ahead of him he wondered what their chances were of success. He had no idea of their destination and he was in an agony of apprehension in case his driver lost the tongah ahead and so missed the boat. He noticed the Malay driver was hissing encouragement at his pony and he added his own hiss, wishing he had a stick to emphasise its message. He was still hissing enthusiastically when at 2 am they came to the village of Panjalanan. In the dark he heard the others climbing from the carts and he and Douglas hurried to join them.

Broome led the way to a long fishing hut where twelve Malays and Chinese lay asleep on wooden berths. They wakened on the entry of the British and after a short conversation the Britishers followed them outside.

The rain had stopped and a clear moon lit the village. Beyond them palm trees ringed the shore and in the moonlight half a mile out the sailing craft that was to take them on the long voyage to Ceylon rode at anchor.

She was a prahu with one short mast and one long, and a thick, high bowsprit. The *Sederhana Djohanis*—the name means 'Simple Jack'—weighed between 25 and 30 tons and was the sort of craft used in native trade up and down the Sumatran coast. She was broad in the beam and bucket-shaped amidships with an 18-inch freeboard. She had a mainsail, a mizzen, staysail and jib but her sails were so thin and worn that the men could see the stars through them. The *Djohanis* was divided in two by a 27-foot-long pent-house which formed the living quarters of the crew. The fore-deck was 8 feet long and 8 feet at its widest. It had a cooking shed forward on the port side. The afterdeck was raised and there was just enough room for the helmsman.

She seemed a frail craft for 18 men with few stores, a single chart, a car radio and a few wrist watches for chronometers to attempt the crossing of 1,500 miles of open sea at the mercy of gales and enemy attack.

The party were taken out to the *Djohanis* in long narrow canoes. Four men to a boat with two paddlers. The boats seemed to Rowley, a non-swimmer, unstable in the extreme as he and Douglas waded first waist deep and then almost shoulder deep towards them. They were hoisted inboard and instinctively Rowley put out his arms in an effort to balance the boat. It brought a stream of anguished Malay from one of the paddlers. Another whispered, 'If the tuan would only sit on his hands, it would be safer for all of us.'

Shamefacedly Rowley did as he was told and when they reached the prahu he was once more helped aboard for his first sight of his new quarters. It was 3 am on 8 March and with a shock Rowley realized it was his thirtieth birthday. Inconsequentially he realised that at last he was now entitled to a marriage allowance. All he had to do was to get to Ceylon to collect it.

Rowley's only sailing experience was in dinghies and the *Djohanis* was well outside his capabilities. But quickly he sensed that the whole tempo of the escape had changed and once again he was not the man who made the decisions. He was little more than a passenger now and among his fellow crewmen he thought he saw the unmistakable qualities of natural leadership.

Ivan Lyon was the first to impress him. Ivan had been seconded from the Gordons to S.O.E. He was an experienced sailor and had done many lone trips in the China Seas. As Rowley watched he pinned a pendulum and a piece of lined paper to the mast. Feeling the gunner's eye upon him Lyon grinned and said, 'If the pendulum goes past that line, we'll turn over.'

Broome, the leader, called them together and told them their statistics of survival. Their food included cases of bully beef, potatoes, carrots, condensed milk, tinned fruit, coffee, tinned butter, biscuits and two boxes of such odds and ends as porridge, pickles, ketchup, curry powder, salt and pepper. In addition they had two sacks of sugar, rice, coconuts and a small quantity of fresh limes and bananas. The *Djohanis* held two large drums each containing sixty gallons of water and there were 80 gallons more in earthenware jars and petrol tins. Reading material consisted of two dog-eared copies of *Esquire* magazines and there was a mixed armoury of two Lewis guns, a few rifles and some revolvers all with an adequate amount of ammunition.

Aboard they found three first-aid tins containing dressings, bandages, M. and B. 693, castor oil, forceps, scissors and morphine; and the men's personal first-aid kits were collected and pooled.

There was a small quantity of sailcloth, thread, sail needles, rope and lengths of bamboo. The prahu had hammers, hatchets, scissors, wire, firewood and a spare charcoal stove. Two hurricane lamps gave light from a mixture of kerosene and coconut oil and there was a stock of flares and flags and a heliograph. Cigarettes, they worked out, were enough for three a day per man with a few one cent cigars and a small store of pipe tobacco. There were five bottles of whisky which they decided would be reserved for medicine only and nine mattresses and blankets to be shared amongst them.

Although there were compasses and a sextant there was no chronometer. They had a chart of the waters round Sumatra and the Indian Ocean and a map from the back of a Gem Dictionary. As auxiliary boats they had a native canoe and two Carley floats.

Under Broome's direction the group split themselves into two watches. Rowley and Douglas found themselves on the same watch, a piece of luck which cheered them greatly. Their watch also included Waller, Davis, the police superintendent, and A. V. Lind, an R.N.V.R. lieutenant who had found the *Djohanis* at Emmerhaven and suggested the escape to Colonel Warren. Lind had been an insurance company executive in Batavia. When war broke out he was mobilised and until the surrender had served in a minesweeper. The other member of Rowley's watch was Lt Brian Passmore, another R.N.V.R. officer who had left his father's printing works at the outbreak of war and until the fall of the Island had worked as an instructor at the School of Demolition in Singapore.

As skipper, Broome did not take a watch, nor did the quartermaster, Jock Campbell, or Doc Davies, the M.O. Chief cook Loo Ngiap Soon, who had been Broome's servant when he was district officer on Christmas Island and his assistant the Malay, Jamal Bin Daim, were both excused. So too was 'Tojo' Clark, the Intelligence Corps lieutenant who was a fluent Japanese linguist and a gifted artist. Three of the Malays who had escorted them aboard agreed to stay with them for a few days, while they remained inside the string of islands which lie off the west coast of Sumatra, to show them the workings of the boat. They were then to make their own way back to Padang.

The port watch was led by Ivan Lyon and included a colourful naval reserve officer called Garth Gorham whose years with the merchant navy off the China coast had given him a contempt of all things Royal Naval which was to upset two other members of his watch, Richard Cox and 'Holly' Holwell, two R.N.V.R. lieutenants. The port watch also included a Dartmouth trained regular sailor, Lt Geoffrey Brooke, and Spanton, the infantry captain Rowley had picked up with Waller in the Indragiri.

They were, he thought, a capable lot and it seemed to him that he could not have picked a better complement than the one that chance and Colonel Warren's eye had brought together.

8

ROWLEY AWOKE the next morning to discover that the boat was already moving between the rocky necklace of islands that are strung round the throat of Padang. He shook Douglas and whispered excitedly,
'We're off.'
The news brought his companion instantly awake and the two men crawled out of the atap-roofed shelter rapidly named by the 18 as the 'pent-house'. It was to be their only protection from the sun and the violent storms they were to encounter in the coming weeks.

Lyon was at the wheel listening intently as the oldest of the three Malays who had come on the boat with them instructed him in the handling of the *Djohanis*. Rowley was struck by the air of quiet authority which radiated from the Gordon Highlander. Self-reliant himself, he recognized a similar quality in Ivan. Although they faced at least a month at the mercy of the Indian Ocean and an uncertain reception in Ceylon, which by the time they arrived might have been invaded by the Japanese, Lyon was wholly engrossed in his sailing lesson. Rowley realized that the man was in his element and thoroughly enjoying himself.

Ivan Lyon was an old hand at long voyages in small craft, mostly alone. Before the war he had sailed from Harwich to Rotterdam in a 12-ton ketch, from Newhaven to Land's End and back in a pilot cutter, from Munich to Dubrovnik in a sailing canoe, from Singapore to Singora in a 3-tonner, from Singapore to Thursday Island, Australia, in a 12-tonner and from Mersing to Saigon in a 3-tonner.

He was a reassuring figure at the helm. Red haired with a clipped red moustache, his spare frame and clear blue eyes radiated energy as he puffed at a chipped and burned briar. He spoke little and in the days to come was to spend many hours staring beyond the line of the horizon into the closed country of his own thoughts. But he was a brave companion and soon the others came to rely implicitly on his judgement and quietly spoken advice.

As he watched, Rowley sensed that Ivan must have had a difficult time in the boarding school atmosphere of his regiment. The Gordons in Singapore were a socially-minded unit and Rowley could not imagine the man at the wheel, glass in hand at a cocktail party with the gossip and small-talk washing round him. In fact Lyon, the son of a Brigadier-General, had left his battalion to become liaison officer to the Chief Censor and had subsequently joined the Free French in a similar job. He had also been Military Secretary to a Cabinet Minister until his selection for special duties.

Jock Campbell, the ex-planter, cut a different figure. Rubicund and paternal, he was to become very much the father of the group, although as its quartermaster he was ruthless in rationing the small store of supplies which he was already packing and checking against a rudimentary manifest.

Broome, the man appointed by Colonel Warren as leader of the party, puzzled Rowley. He was a taciturn man given to long periods of withdrawal and in the days to come his methods were to exasperate the impetuous gunner. They were from vastly different stables. Rowley was a fighting soldier trained in the profession of arms, Broome a Cambridge-educated career civil servant. Fluent in French, Cantonese and Malay, Broome, after service in China and the Chinese

Protectorate in Malaya, had been a District Officer on Christmas Island and the bureaucratic methods he learned there were not calculated to endear him to the unorthodox gunner.

One by one as they wakened, the other members of the company joined Rowley and Douglas on the deck, yawning and rubbing away the sleep from their eyes.

The first to come out was Lind, the R.N.V.R. lieutenant. Public School background notwithstanding, Lind was markedly left in his political views and his heated arguments with Rowley were to do much to enliven the trip in the days ahead. But on this first morning he was intent only on lessons in handling the *Djohanis* and, after an envious glance at Ivan at the wheel, he was soon in a deep conversation in racy Malay with one of the fishermen.

Waller, the Gunner major who was the next on deck, was quick to make his first claim for the title of friendly pessimist which he held successfully against all-comers for the rest of the voyage. He looked with quiet disparagement at the battered prahu, winced at the threadbare sails and shook his head slowly. 'Doesn't look as if she'll last the day out,' he said mournfully. But Rowley noticed that he too was quick to lend a hand to the Malays as they trimmed ship and to listen without interruption to their instructions.

Davis and Passmore, the next two men up, presented interesting studies. Davis, a Superintendent in the Malayan Police, possessed a self-assurance that was majestic and although his knowledge of sailing was perhaps less extensive than that of Ivan Lyon, he did not hesitate to advise forcefully on many questions of seamanship. He had a magnificent physique and he was soon doing the work of two men on the little ship.

Passmore was, at 42, the oldest member of the crew. He was a gangling six-footer who almost brought the atap roof down as he hit it with his head coming out on to the deck. It was to be his unlucky lot to endure frequent injury during the trip from collisions with the ship's meagre furniture. This was

Passmore's second war; he had been a Pilot Officer in France in 1918.

All the time the men had been getting to know each other the *Djohanis* had been dancing across the sea in sparkling style. By noon she had taken them 33 miles along the coast towards the outer islands from which they would begin their dangerous ocean crossing.

Douglas leaned on the stern bulkhead and watched the beaches of the mainland sweep by. In the brilliant sunshine the long green silence of the forest of palms which fringed the edges of the sands looked cool and inviting. It was difficult to believe that somewhere in the island behind them in deep forests or on the slopes of the mountains that crowded the lowlands into the sea, a Japanese army was advancing, killing and burning as it marched. The invasion of Sumatra had been swift, deadly and completely successful. The Japanese had swept over the island crushing the small forces which were available to defend the country. Soon they were masters of the entire land and they swarmed through the streets of Padang, scooping up the servicemen who had undergone so many privations and dangers to escape them. The *Djohanis* had sailed in the nick of time.

It still seemed incredible to Douglas that only a few short weeks before, he had been trapped on Singapore Island, apparently at the mercy of that same army. With sudden optimism he looked forward to their landing in Ceylon and he made up his mind to get back into the fight as soon after their arrival as he could.

Rowley too was thinking about Singapore, and his memories were bitter. In three years he had built up a comfortable home on the Island and when he left the Brigadier's quarters at No. 4 Royal Road he had been forced to abandon everything he loved. His dogs, the horses, his car, the furniture he had collected, all were gone. Before he closed the door for the last time, Rowley had looked round his home at the books and pictures he had bought and the silver cups he had

1. A lithograph of the *Sederhana Djohanis*.

2. Hour after hour the watch swept the horizon through binoculars straining for the sight of a merchantman or a British warship. For 36 days until they reached the coast of Ceylon they looked in vain.

3. His crew-mates watch as Rowley, in his Jermyn Street trilby prepares for his hazardous climb along the bowsprit. In a mounting storm it was his job to haul in the jib sail.

4. After days of drifting the *Djohanis* at last catches the tail of the monsoon which will take her to the coast of Ceylon.

won riding races, all the hundred and one things that go to make a comfortable home in the Far East. He was a man who loved possessions and it had hurt him bitterly to leave his home for the Japanese to loot. His most treasured things, including a gold cigarette case and a pair of ivory hair-brushes which had belonged to his father, an Infantry Major who had been killed at Gallipoli in 1915, he packed into a small suitcase, but that too had been lost when he abandoned the junk. Now everything he owned was in the small technical haversack at his side.

At first when he thought of all that had gone he was depressed. But the sun was shining, the wind fresh, and the sea was alive with golden points of light. The *Djohanis* was carving curved shavings of foam from its surface and scudding under a wind from exactly the right direction and soon the depression lifted and Rowley felt a lightening of heart and spirit. His possessions had gone and there was no use worrying about them. He was on his way to freedom and after the hopelessness of the early days in Padang when it seemed they would never escape, it was a delight to have a purpose again. He was alive and the only things he had to worry about were himself, his pistol and the contents of his haversack. He grinned and moved off to meet the other members of the party.

Rowley was immediately drawn to Spanton, the Manchester Regiment captain who was at that moment clipping his splendid auburn moustache at the door of the pent-house. Rowley marvelled at the man's neatness. His khaki drill had taken a severe drubbing since he and Waller had 'requisitioned' a rowing boat from the Raffles Hotel and carried it to the shore with the intention of rowing to Sumatra. But it was neatly darned and brushed and the rest of his equipment shone in the sunshine. By his side 'Tojo' Clark, the son of an Englishman and a Japanese mother, looked defiantly unmilitary as he sketched the *Djohanis* on a pad of scrap paper.

'Tojo's' career had been varied. Born and educated in Yokohama he had been forced to leave Japan when the surveillance by the political police became unbearable. In Malaya he joined the R.A.S.C. as a private soldier. He was commissioned into the Intelligence Corps a year later and employed as a Japanese interpreter and tutor. On 13 February he left Malaya with a boatload of Japanese prisoners but within twenty-four hours their ship had been dive-bombed and beached on a waterless desert island. 'Tojo' had island-hopped in small boats until he reached the Indragiri where Lt-Commander Terry, one of the three skippers from Rowley's base at Rengat, had picked him up and brought him to safety.

The *Djohanis*' medical officer was, like Rowley, a Welshman, Major L. E. C. ('Bill') Davies. The ship in which he had been evacuated was also dive-bombed but he was picked up by a gunboat and brought to Tembilahan and the first stage of the 'Tourist Route'. The 'doc' combined his medical duties with odd jobs like cleaning the ship's bilges and acting as junior quartermaster to Jock whose keen sense of humour he shared. Professionally the voyage excited him since it gave him the opportunity to study the health of the other men under stress and he kept a detailed diary of the crew, their reactions and their physical condition during the long haul across the Indian Ocean.

To his chagrin, Lt Geoffrey A. G. Brooke, the only Royal Navy regular aboard the *Djohanis*, was the Doc's first patient when he became the only member of the crew to be seasick during the voyage. Brooke, at 22 the baby of the crew, was appalled. He was a Dartmouth cadet who had already been at sea for two years when the war started and his record of active service was formidable. He was on H.M.S. *Prince of Wales* when she was severely damaged during the sinking of the *Bismark* in 1941 when H.M.S. *Hood* also went down. Later in the same year he sailed in the *Prince of Wales* when she took Winston Churchill to meet President Roosevelt and when the *Prince of Wales* was sunk by Japanese dive-bombers off Kuantan on 10 December, Brooke survived to organize a ferry service in Penang until that island too was evacuated. He was dive-bombed for a second time when the ship in which he was being evacuated was sunk in the Rhiu Archipelago. He finally reached Sumatra in a junk. That he should be a martyr to sea-sickness after such a saga, though it was a weakness he shared with Nelson, seemed to him a disaster beyond belief.

Garth Gorham's hoot of derision heightened his embarrassment. Garth who navigated the *Djohanis* was an ex-Merchant Navy second mate with a magnificent black beard and a fiery eye. His contempt of all things Royal Naval from the Fleet in port to the flowers in Admirals' cabins, was withering and delivered in a booming voice that filled the ship. His views, thought Rowley, were delivered with all the heat, fire and smoke of the volcano he so closely resembled. But he proved himself an admirable navigator although he had only a map torn from an atlas, a wrist watch for a chronometer and an unreliable radio to help him. An archetypal Yorkshireman, who held a Master's ticket with the Brocklebank Line, he had shipped out with the Indo-China Steam Navigation Company for service in the China Seas. His distaste for things Royal Naval was probably formed when the Admiralty took over his river boat and he was sent to Singapore on an advance base ship. Garth, or Columbus, as, inevitably, he came to be called, was bombed three times before he arrived in Sumatra. Yet not even those calamities shook his deep-seated belief that the real enemy of all merchant sailors was the Royal Navy.

It was not a philosophy which commended him to Richard Cox or 'Holly' Holywell, both of them lieutenants and touchily proud of the 'Wavy Navy' in which they served. Cox, who had sailed to the Baltic and back as a boy in a four masted schooner, and Holly, were companions of long standing. Cox with his slickly brilliantined hair was always immaculate and the naval counterpart of Spanton. He had enlisted in the R.N.V.R. in 1939 from a Weymouth shipping office and served in mine-sweepers round the Malayan and Singapore coasts all through the campaign. When the island at last fell, Cox was first officer on H.M.S. *Trang* where he met Holly.

Holly joined the *Trang* after a year on the staff of the Extended Defence Officer in Singapore. White bearded, he was the second oldest member of the ship's company and like Passmore had served in the R.A.F. in the last year of World War One. Between wars he worked on plantations in Malaya until he was mobilised into the R.N.V.R. on the outbreak of the Second World War.

The two men sailed together in the *Trang* from Singapore on the fatal Friday, 13th, but she ran aground and after she was refloated developed engine trouble. She was scuttled and the two men found themselves sitting side by side in a ship's lifeboat. Holly and Cox were at sea together for ten days before they landed on Pulau Sinkep where they commandeered a motor boat and escaped to Sumatra.

There were two natives on the *Djohanis*. Loo Ngiap Soon was a Chinese who had been Broome's servant since his days as a District Officer on Christmas Island. He was appointed cook and the other native, Jamal Bin Daim, who had been Supt Davis' driver in the Malayan police, became his assistant. But it was their second job which won them the respect of the others on the *Djohanis*. In the event of attack by Japanese aircraft they were to make themselves as conspicuous as possible on the deck in the hope that the Japanese would mistake their oriental skins for those of local fishermen.

By the time the *Djohanis* dropped anchor on the night of 9 March everyone on the ship had come to know each other and friendships that were to last throughout the war were beginning to form and flower. That night on the foredeck in the velvet dark of the night a club was formed which if it lacked the facilities of its counterparts in St James's had equally strict requirements of its exclusive membership of six. To be accepted into the Fo'c'sle club, three talents were necessary. A member had to be able to sing, argue and tell stories. Rowley was an inevitable choice and Holly, Campbell, Douglas Fraser, Cox and 'Doc' Davies, the other members, were hard-pressed to combat his outrageous views on almost every subject under the sun. By popular consent Holly was chairman. With his venerable white beard and his quiet sensible voice he was the only man who could silence the ebullient gunner and he had, in addition, a rare talent for racy songs which endeared him to the membership.

Riding without lights on the rim of the jagged white coral reefs in a calm sea the men passed the evening talking quietly of their days in Singapore. Their supper, though meagre, had been better fare than any of them had been accustomed to over the past weeks and they were united in their praise of the marvels that Soon had worked with the rice. With contented stomachs they stretched on the deck under a moon that was pure Hollywood and let themselves be lulled by the movement of the *Djohanis* and the wet chop of the sea as it slapped at her sides. They felt strangely secure in their wooden world and an age away from the horrors they had left behind them in their trek across the East Indies.

The first 'Sumatra' they were to experience at sea blew up at 4.30 am the next morning. Although by comparison with later storms it was a mild one it showed sufficient teeth to be alarming.

All of the men on the *Djohanis* were used to these sudden tropical storms born in the mountains that form the rocky backbone of the island. In Singapore the sudden banging of the shutters of their homes in the early dawn had been warning enough to rouse them and send them on hasty slippered tours closing windows and doors. Back in bed they had listened as the wind howled and the rain made knife thrusts at the atap roofs of their bungalows and then, when it ended as dramatically as it had begun, they padded round opening the windows again. It was a pleasant ritual.

But in a frail wooden boat in range of the menacing bite of the coral's jagged jaws the men on the boat watched the storm's caprice with wary eyes. The friendly slap of the water at the side of the boat changed to an angry pummelling. The suddenly petulant sea erupted violently and the Malay fishermen called to each other as they scurried round fumbling with the sheets.

It was no friendly wind now, fussing round their bungalows. Like a kettle coming suddenly to boil the 'Sumatra' blew in a fury that made the sea bubble. The decks pitched and ran with rain that made them glossy and unsafe. In a moment the men were soaked with the cold rain and could feel the chill eating into their bones.

The *Djohanis* was making considerable way on the skirts of the wind when the Malay skipper saw the white grin of coral ahead. Douglas detected more than normal urgency in his voice as he screamed into the wind his orders to go about. The *Djohanis* was difficult to bring round and skidded on the water, stern down like a tin tray on a snow slope, as she turned, protesting. Rowley thought what a pig she would be to handle.

The men watched anxiously as the coral reefs grew nearer. Everyone knew that if the *Djohanis* struck their escape, if not their lives would be over. Not even the most powerful swimmer among them could have fought his way through the boiling seas to safety. And even if by some incredible good fortune they could have reached the reef the sea would pluck them off again with ease.

Under their feet they could feel the timbers of the *Djohanis* groaning in protest as the winds and the waves fought to control her. For a time it seemed that their contrary demands would do the coral's work for it and rip them asunder. Beneath them the seas crashed and heaved whilst around them and above in the rigging the winds roared and ripped at the canvas. Clinging to whatever support they could find the white men watched the nimble Malays fighting their battle with an old enemy.

It struck Rowley that soon it would be their turn to fight in this terrifying arena and he watched as the Malays worked so that when his turn came he would be able to take on the adversary with at least some knowledge of what he was doing.

A sickening crash disturbed his concentration. He looked up and saw to his dismay that the boom had fractured under the force of the wind. It dangled uselessly like a broken arm but in a moment a Malay was swarming along it from the mast with a length of rope to lash the splintered wood together. It was an amazing feat and Rowley watched with admiration.

In the excitement of the moment the men on the *Djohanis* had forgotten about the reefs. Now they saw that they had missed them and at last the Malays brought the *Djohanis* into a safe anchorage off a small, deserted island. Only then when the danger was over did Rowley and the others realise how tired they were. After a hastily prepared supper they crawled under the atap shelter and slept fitfully until they were awakened by the sun streaming through the pent-house door.

That day the Malays left them near the anchorage. As they watched them scramble over the side the men felt a moment's unease, but Broome took advantage of the anchorage to get everyone working and to ship fresh water. Under the blazing sun at sea he knew the men were going to need all the liquid they could collect if they were to survive. The task completed Broome looked at Ivan Lyon at the wheel. His obvious impatience to be off was infectious. Broome called to the others. 'Time we were moving.' Obediently they made their way to their positions on the boat. He ordered, 'Anchor up' and the *Djohanis* was away across the empty acres of an unknown ocean.

Their great adventure had begun. Behind them lay the wreckage of the Malayan campaign and a victorious Japanese Army was even at that moment swarming over Sumatra and the places they had just left. Rengat, the rubber factory, the railhead and the hotel in Padang, they would all be Japanese Army camps by now. There was no going back for any of them. Their escape bid would be enough in itself to give the Japanese the excuse to shoot them; at best they would be herded into a prison camp for the rest of the war.

But the perils that lay ahead were only marginally less appalling. They did not know when they might run into a Japanese ship or be spotted by one of the enemy's daily air patrols over the Indian Ocean. Even if they succeeded in crossing the Indian Ocean they were not sure of linking up with their own side in Ceylon. The speed of the Japanese advance through Malaya made anything seem possible, even the fall of India.

But for the moment at least they were free, they were taking positive action and they were heading in what they hoped was the right direction for freedom. They had no choice but to let events take their own course.

At the wheel Ivan inwardly praised the native builders of the boat. Now she had a following wind her mood had changed and she answered all his commands like a well-schooled pony. She was responsive and deft and her eagerness in the water was warming. Under the freshening wind she was soon scudding merrily towards the outer islands now on the horizon. It seemed incredible that a boat which could behave so well in favourable conditions could become so instantly unresponsive the moment she was asked to go to windward.

To Douglas the charm of the voyage so far was marred by one misgiving. They were heading in quite the wrong direction and he was relieved when the wind changed and the *Djohanis* turned unwillingly on to the other tack. Next he began to worry about the sails. They were so threadbare they were translucent and it seemed impossible that they could stand up to the sort of weather which the night before had fractured the boom with such ease. He glanced at them anxiously as he felt the force of the wind increase on his back. They were stretched like threadbare trousers, straining at every seam. He was not surprised when the filled sail suddenly ripped in a gash that swept down its straining belly like a sabre slash and in a moment the *Djohanis* became sluggish and wayward.

'Blast,' said Ivan. 'I'm afraid we'll have to heave to. No use trying to repair a sail at night.'

An anchor was dropped and Douglas watched it break the clear blue water in a lace of spray as it plunged to the sand bottom below.

That night it was his watch with Rowley. To their disgust they had been posted as look-outs on the prow.

'Look-outs,' whispered Rowley, bitterly. 'I couldn't see a Jap if he swarmed up the anchor rope. And it's only a bloody sentry's job anyway.'

He brushed at his moustache in angry impatience. 'I don't know about you, Douglas, but I'm off to sleep.' He huddled under the prow and within seconds gentle snores were serenading the ocean about them, filling the vacuum of the dying wind. Douglas decided that his wisest course would be to join him and soon he too was asleep wooing the ocean with troubador trumpetings.

Daybreak found the *Djohanis* only five miles west of Pegagu and when they awoke the men were dismayed to find that they had been brought to within a very few miles of their starting point. Waller voiced the fears of them all.

'By the time we get to Ceylon the war will be over,' he said.

'Possibly,' replied Broome dryly, 'but if we don't repair these sails we won't get there at all.'

To Rowley's disgust he handed out sailing needles to all hands.

'I can't sew,' said Rowley hotly. 'I always prick my finger.'

Fraser looked with a grin at the lethal sail needle which Rowley was brandishing. 'I wouldn't worry,' he said. 'If you prick your finger with that thing it will be fatal and your worries will be over.'

With a bad grace Rowley sat cross-legged and pulled the sail towards him. Davis and Douglas joined him and picked up their needles and began to sew. To his annoyance Rowley saw that Douglas was sewing deftly in comparison with his own somewhat clumsy stitches and Davis was stitching with his usual air of competent authority. He was glad when at last the sail was finished and it was hauled back into position.

Rowley stood back to admire their handiwork. He had never seen a sail so thin and he had little hope of it lasting. It did not. Within minutes of them setting sail they heard the familiar ripping sound and once again the sail had to be hauled down and re-stitched.

Their second efforts were more successful. Rowley looked dubiously at the sail as it bellied out under the strengthening wind but the stitches held and the *Djohanis* shuddered as she felt its strength.

By now they had been on the *Djohanis* for nearly three days and they looked with longing at the little island ahead of them. They could see a fishing village on its shore and to them it seemed a metropolis. Hurriedly they made preparations to go ashore and as they worked they watched three prahus which came into the anchorage under Malay crews. It seemed to the Doc that allowing for their greater familiarity the Malays made no better job of handling their craft than Ivan on the *Djohanis* and it gave him confidence for the days ahead.

They took it in turns to go ashore and wandered round the village buying limes and bananas from the traders in the market. They could not find sailcloth but from their pooled store of 628 guilders they bought a bolt of deck-chair canvas to patch their sails.

To Rowley's disgust the whole of the rest of the day was spent repairing the sails and rigging of their boat. With rope they had bought ashore they replaced the worst sections of the rigging and the patches of deck-chair canvas made passable replacements for sail-cloth. It was long work and for Rowley, at least, tedious in the extreme. But a diversion was near. They had been sitting for what seemed hours under a broiling sun and his temper was worsening when across the water from the north of the island they heard the sound of a marine engine.

They knew they were in Jap waters and it was only to be expected that a patrol vessel would sooner or later come upon them. In a second the warm security of their small world had been shattered and Rowley regretted he had ever complained about such mundane tasks as sewing the sails.

Broome whispered an order, 'Jamal, Soon, get up on the tiller and make yourselves as conspicuous as possible. The rest of you follow me.'

Crouching below the level of the gunwale he made his way over to the penthouse and the others joined him, carrying their weapons. Rowley was glad to feel the reassurance of his Thompson and looked around at his companions. Obviously they shared a common idea. After so many adventures they were determined not to be taken prisoner at this late hour. He thought with grim amusement of the surprise in store for the Japs when they boarded this innocent-looking fishing-boat.

Broome was squinting through the covering over the door. 'It's a tug,' he said, 'towing a barge. Doesn't look as though she's armed, but she's flying no flag.'

He turned to the men lined up behind him. 'I'm afraid the chances are that she's Japanese.'

An urgent whisper from the tiller brought Broome back to the door. It was Soon.

'The tug has anchored, sir. She's putting off a boat. There seems to be only one man in her...'

'Poor sod,' thought Rowley, grimly.

He was startled when Soon next spoke. He made no effort to lower his voice and it must have carried across the water between the two boats. But the words reassured him. 'It's all right, it's a European and he's going ashore.'

There was relief in the penthouse as the arms were once again stacked against the inner planking of the boat and the men scrambled out on to the deck to see the craft that had so dramatically interrupted their peaceful sewing session. Broome was staring over the water at the boat that was pulling away from the tug.

'He's a white man, all right,' he said, 'and I've been thinking that we might be able to borrow a chart of these islands from him if he's got any spares.'

He turned to Lind. 'You'd better take the canoe and go ashore and try to make contact with him,' he said. He stepped into the penthouse and when he returned he was carrying one of the precious bottles of whisky.

'Here,' he said, handing it to Lind. 'No harm in a few trading goods. Let's see if the natives are friendly.'

9

LIND STEPPED into the dinghy clutching the precious bottle of whisky. It represented one fifth of their total liquor supply and he was aware of the anxiety of the others until he had stowed it safely in the bottom of the boat.

From ashore the European had been watching the activity aboard the *Djohanis*, his eyes shaded with his hand against the bright sunlight, and as Lind dipped his oars he began to walk down the beach towards the water's edge. Bent over the oars Lind sent the dinghy cutting through the surf until he felt her rock under the grip of the stranger who had waded out to meet him. He nodded, jumped over the side and together the two men pulled the dinghy on to the beach. Lind grinned at the sudden light in the stranger's eye when he saw the whisky in the bottom of the boat.

'A very welcome sight, mynheer,' said the other in a thick Dutch accent, nodding at the whisky. He towered over Lind and the hand he stretched out in greeting ended in fingers fat as croissants.

Lind's uniform was creased and worn. During the first anxious days on the *Djohanis* there had been little opportunity for shaving and a dark stubble shaded his chin. But his manners were impeccable and with a formal grace that would have done credit to a Naval ward room he reached into the boat and brought out the bottle.

'I wonder if you'd care for a spot?' he said. He paused in apology. 'I'm afraid there aren't any glasses...'

The Dutchman's laugh was born in the great cavern of his belly and the palm fronds seemed to rustle in its wake as it echoed across the empty beach.

'Glasses?' he roared, reaching out for the bottle and uncorking it in practised synchronization. 'Who needs glasses?'

Lind watched the level of the whisky dropping dramatically as the Dutchman drank. After an incredibly long time the Dutchman lowered the bottle, wiped its neck and passed it over to Lind. His eyes were watering from the fire of the spirit but as a whisky drinker he was obviously first eleven material. Lind nodded his thanks and took the bottle uncertainly. It had been some time since he had tasted liquor and after the Dutchman's performance he felt hopelessly outclassed. But he took a deep breath and raised the whisky to his lips.

'Thank you,' he murmured. 'Cheers.'

The first taste burned his mouth and lit raging fires in his throat. His head was suddenly light and he fought back a wave of nausea. But when he lowered the bottle the Dutchman was grinning his approval.

'Drinking is good?' he asked.

Lind sank gently to the beach, gripping the sand with his fist.

'Oh yes,' he said gamely. 'Nothing better. Er... won't you sit down?'

With an amiable grunt, hugging the bottle to his chest the giant Dutchman squatted at his side and after more whisky he asked,

'Escaping from the Japs?'

Lind nodded. 'We're hoping to cross to Ceylon,' he said. 'We thought you might be able to let us have some charts of the reefs and the outer islands. We don't know these waters and our Malays would not take us any further.'

The Dutchman was shocked. 'Charts? I not need charts.

Like the bloddy front of my 'and I know these waters. Charts? Charts we forget.'

Charts having been dismissed with the contempt that he had earlier shown for glasses, the Dutchman took another long pull at the whisky. Then he pointed dramatically at his chest. 'I be your chart. I bring you through the islands and the coral reefs. I give you big tow with my boat. Is O.K.?' He beamed good-will.

Lind beamed back. 'Is bloody marvellous,' he said.

The Dutchman laughed and his face purpled with effort as he leaned over and gripped Lind's shoulder.

'Is bloddy marvellous,' he repeated. Then he paused. There was serious work afoot.

'Now we better drink whisky, no?' he said anxiously.

The journey back to the boat seemed longer to Lind than had the row to the shore. The oars were behaving badly and his feet showed a tendency to slip so that twice he found he was struggling to prevent himself from falling into the bottom of the boat. It was all irresistibly funny and he was still giggling when he was helped aboard the *Djohanis*.

'He's stoned,' he heard someone exclaim in envy. 'He's drunk the blasted whisky himself.'

With tipsy dignity Lind raised a hand to quell the howls of protest.

'Quite the contrary,' he told them benignly. 'I've just met this absolutely charming Dutchman.' He paused. 'And he is going to give us a tow.'

The Dutchman waited until late in the day and any possible air activity minimised; then as the men on the sailing boat watched he rowed back to his tug which was moored some distance from the shore. They heard the engines cough into life and crowded to the rail as the tug steamed alongside.

From the wheelhouse the Dutchman waved a greeting.

'Ready for a rope?' he called.

Broome waved back his assent and a line from the tug was made fast to the prow of the *Djohanis*.

After the heat and general activity of the day it was pleasant to lie on deck while the tug towed them through the sea, free of the responsibility of navigation and the impulsive winds. Their prow set up white brackets of foam and the men busied themselves stowing stores and cleaning their weapons. The familiar rituals of military life soothed the soldiers and the sailors felt the old satisfaction of a deck moving beneath their feet.

But, as they watched, the sky darkened and the wind that had cooled their faces became cold and sullen. White edges showed on the rims of the sea-swell and the masts creaked as the sails tightened and strained. The Sumatra, when it came, pummelled the sailing boat and the tug in front of them dipped crazily as it disappeared in the valleys of a rising sea. The couchant wave crests became rampant and angry and dragged their blue, lace-edged robes high into the air to crash down over the gunwales of the *Djohanis*. The ship pitched and bucketed and the men's few possessions, so carefully stowed, were scattered and soaked in the palm-roofed penthouse.

Like a sledge drawn by runaway horses the *Djohanis* was dragged, curvetting wildly through the mounting seas, by the thick black hawser from the tug which strained as though at any moment it would break. Buffetted and slithering about the deck the men grabbed at any hand-hold that would prevent them from being washed over the side. Clutching frantically at the rigging with the spray beating at his knuckles Douglas felt as though he were hanging on to the lash of a bull-whip while next to him Rowley spat sea-water and cursed with quiet fluency. He had never experienced a storm at once so beautiful and so chilling in its strength as this. In the lightning he could see the land in sharp detail. He thought of firework displays on festivals and holidays in Singapore and of chill Novembers in Wales when, as a small boy, he had watched a ragged Guy burn on the bonfire in the park. The thought of his house of warm red brick and long, lazy

5. Aboard the *Sederhana Djohanis* – *left to right*: Bill Waller, Garth Gorham, Davis and Lind.

6. Chinaman Loo Ngiap Soon (left) and his Malayan companion Jamal Bin Daim were human camouflage during the long trip across the Indian Ocean. When the *Djohanis* was 'buzzed' by Jap aircraft it was their job to stand on the deck in the hope that the enemy would think them innocent fishermen.

7. Empty, her jib-sail drooping forlornly, the *Djohanis* lies alongside the *Anglo-Canadian*.

evenings before a huge log fire in the lime boudoir at Bodrhyddan shut out the storm. He settled as comfortably as he could and waited for the Sumatra to die.

All through that night the Dutchman, a Wagnerian figure in the flickering light of his wheelhouse, now vanishing in a trough only to reappear on a crest of wild water, towed them through angry seas until at length the wind subsided.

In calmer waters the tug towed them into the lee of a small island, Pulau Ilir. The Dutchman had brought them 65 miles nearer Ceylon and now his tug cut a crescent of foam as he turned and came alongside.

'Is as far as I go,' he called. 'Now you be all right, no?'

Broome shouted back his thanks and the Dutchman told him.

'There are more reefs ahead but do not worry. You be all right. Soon you see Plyades lighthouse, though maybe no light there now. Watch for Japs. Then open sea. Ceylon only 1,200 maybe 1,400 miles ahead.'

He made it sound like round the corner, thought Gorham who was to navigate.

As he was shouting his instructions the Dutchman was moving about the deck of his tug, searching. At last he found what he wanted. He bent, straightened and then his great shoulders swung as he sent a coil of stout rope whistling through the air to land with a wet thud on the deck of the *Djohanis*.

'Liddle present. When war is over you come back. I give you plenty whisky.'

He waved. The white water churned under his propeller and he was away. The last they heard was his great laugh rolling across the water towards them.

'What an extraordinarily nice chap,' murmured Spanton. 'I do hope he's going to be all right.'

Lind watched the tug until its outline became a distant blur.

'I think he'll manage,' he said.

No bigger than an English meadow the island of Pulau

Ilir looked enchanting from the deck of the *Djohanis*. In the centre of the island a small hill peeked above the circle of trees and in the morning sun a spring which ran from its shoulder glinted silver and inviting. The men on the boat watched it with longing. The spring argued a pool of fresh water where they could bathe and wash the irritating salt from the previous night's storm from their bodies and their grubby and stained clothing.

Broome, as excited as any, marshalled them into shore-going parties and Rowley and Douglas waited impatiently, suddenly aware of the cramped surroundings of the *Djohanis*. They longed to walk on dry land. When at length it was their turn to go ashore they scrambled into the dinghy like freed schoolboys and craned over the shoulder of Davis who was rowing them for a closer look at the island. Davis steadied the dinghy in the surf and grinned at the haste with which the two leapt out into the waist deep water and wading and stumbling made their way to the beach. The sand was hot and sharp on their bare feet and the sun tightened the salt skin on their backs as they ploughed up to the palms and scrub which surrounded the hill. Somewhere in its deep, green heart they could hear the sound of the stream as it poured into the pool. The scrub tore at their legs but they ignored it in their haste to reach the water.

Suddenly Douglas saw that Rowley who had gone ahead had stopped and to his astonishment was dancing and slapping at his body. 'Bloody mosquitoes,' he roared. 'The bloody island's alive.'

Douglas soon felt them them attack. A thousand needles bit at every inch of bare skin and he too hopped and howled as more insects swarmed over him. His skin crawled and his hair was alive with tiny irritating bodies. He grimaced in distaste as, scratching and slapping, he caught up with Rowley.

'Let's get it over with and get back on board,' he said.

The pool, when they reached it, looked cool and inviting

but their mood had been shattered. They jumped in and bathed hurriedly, and as they soaked and scrubbed at their clothes they worried about the gauntlet of insect bites they would have to run before they reached the safety of the boat.

The return journey was even worse than the arrival had been. Their urgent scratching had drawn pin pricks of blood which attracted fresh flights of mosquitoes and by the time they had scrambled back into the dinghy their whole bodies were on fire and swollen from the bites.

It was maddening, a mocking finale to a dream of desert islands that had lasted since boyhood. As they paddled out into the bay Rowley turned back to glare at the treacherous paradise behind them.

'The first thing I shall do when I get home,' he told Douglas with venomous solemnity, 'is to strangle a travel agent. Desert islands!'

Aboard the *Djohanis* they found that preparations to sail were already under way. The whole crew shared a desire to put a large stretch of the Indian Ocean between them and Pulau Ilir as quickly as they could. It was a view that both Douglas and Rowley endorsed and they joined in the work with enthusiasm. Soon they were under way and the island dropped behind them.

That night the storm hit them with renewed fury, lashing at bodies which ached with tiredness and the strain of the previous night's gale. But this time they had no tug to help them and the *Djohanis* pitched and rolled, utterly defenceless at the mercy of wind and wave. Worse, the exhausting litany of the four hour watch was beginning to tell on men already worn out from the weeks of retreat from Singapore. As Rowley scrambled out to join his watch his body ached and he looked up at the threadbare fore-sails straining in the wind in sick apprehension at the thought of another dispiriting sewing bee.

Broome saw his glance and nodded in agreement at Rowley's worried look.

'I don't think they're going to take much more,' he said and for a moment he was silent. Then he spoke again.

'I suppose you realize that one of us is going to have to get the bloody things down.'

Rowley had forgotten the struggle the Malays had undergone to release the torn mainsail so that it could be repaired. It was a hell of a prospect and he did not envy the man who was chosen. He was relieved when Broome added, 'I don't mind going up the mainmast if I have to,' but he felt the first stirrings of apprehension when Broome went on, 'What we need is someone with really strong leg muscles to go along the bowsprit to bring in the jib.'

He paused again as an idea struck him and then he turned to Rowley.

'You used to do a lot of riding, didn't you? I remember seeing you on Singapore racecourse.'

Rowley nodded. He had an unpleasant notion of what was coming next.

'As I see it you've got the best chance of any of us on the bowsprit then. You must have strong leg muscles and success is all a matter of being able to grip the mast with your knees and edging along until you reach the jib. To someone with riding muscles it shouldn't be all that difficult.

Rowley looked in horror at the bowsprit which stretched out and up into the noisy night ahead of them. It looked like a young tree as it dipped and waved in the storm. Climbing along it would be difficult enough in a calm sea, he thought. At night in a gale with the added hazard of driving rain it would be almost impossible to keep a grip.

He looked round at Broome who had followed his thoughts.

'I'm afraid if you do slip that's it. There is no way we can turn about to pick you up. We'd have to leave you.'

There was no point in complaining. He had been elected and he would just have to make the best job of it he could; he tried not to think of falling into the boiling sea and being swept away in the waves. He turned to Douglas who was standing a little behind and had heard Broome's proposal. His face was shocked and he looked at Rowley anxiously. Rowley nodded his thanks for Douglas' silent sympathy, but he accepted Broome's reasoning.

By now the gale was in full throat and it could only be minutes before the sails split under its attack. Broome looked at him:

'No time like the present,' he shouted above the wind.

Once more Rowley looked up at the bowsprit, the tip of which was lost in darkness and rain. It looked bigger and wider every moment and he knew that even a moment's relaxation of his grip would send him plunging into the sea.

Douglas spoke. His voice was strained.

'Sure you can make it?' he asked.

Rowley found a tight grin and hurriedly pinned it to his face. 'No,' he said, shortly, 'but I don't see any alternative.' He pushed his way up to the prow, bending against the gale, his worn shorts tugging at his leg, outlining the hard muscles. To the others watching from the shelter of the penthouse he looked a lonely figure, his hair flying in the wind.

As he reached the pole, he bent to take a grip of the stays that lashed it to the ship. Half-crouched, he turned and waved and the men behind him waved back, helpless to give him aid. He threw a leg over the bowsprit and taking a deep breath began slowly to edge forward but as he left the shelter of the hull the force of the wind struck at him. His breath gone from him, he swayed and his hand slipped on the wet timber of the mast. Before he could renew his grip he had fallen forward until he was stretched full length, both arms twined round the mast as he fought to regain his balance. The sea rushed under him and for a moment every sense was deadened by the sound of its angry roar. He closed his eyes and with an effort steadied himself against the spar. Instinctive messages flashed from his brain summoning his muscles to their work and slowly, unwillingly he forced his body back until he was once again upright. 'It's like the bloody Dunmow Flitch,' he thought, 'and I'm the bacon.'

Slowly his breath came back and he steadied himself until he found his point of balance, half-crouched over the mast like a steeplechase jockey. It wasn't unlike riding a wet and restive horse, he thought, and he thanked God for his riding muscles. Tentatively he put his hands further up the mast and took a firm grasp as far ahead as he could reach without losing his balance. Cautiously he edged his body forward, his legs tightening round the mast as the *Djohanis* bucked beneath him. It was easier, he found, to move forward as the bows came up on a wave, pressing his weight against the spar, but in the trough that followed he had to hang helplessly as the spar plunged down beneath him.

Minutes passed and as he found a rhythm he moved on with greater assurance. It was better, he discovered, if he didn't look down and he concentrated on the jib sail which, as Ivan Lyon brought the boat momentarily into the wind, flapped like wet tripe ahead of him. It seemed an eternity until he reached the bowsprit stays and he rested before leaning down to furl the sodden sail-cloth.

That was the worst time. He had to grab the sail with both hands and only his legs kept him anchored to his uncertain perch. A sudden gust of wind now and he would have spun helplessly into the water below.

He had taken short lengths of rope with him inside his shirt and one by one he drew them out to wrap them round the sail when he had furled it. At last he was finished and he began the difficult backward journey to the deck. It seemed to last for hours. The rain ran down his face, blinding him, and his muscles were weakening in the soaking cold of the storm. He forced himself to work slowly, resisting the impulse to rush to the safety of the ship but at last he felt the grip of hands steadying the last inches of his journey. Soon he was standing, uncertainly, on the fo'c'sle, swaying as his muscles slackened, the centre of a grinning and admiring group.

'Bloody good show,' said Douglas gripping Rowley's arm in his delight at his safe return and when Broome came up to join them he patted Rowley's shoulder. 'Well done,' he said. 'I'm sure the rest of your watch won't mind if you turn in and get warm.'

From his perch behind the wheel Ivan Lyon watched him making his way uncertainly along the deck towards the penthouse; Rowley saw him and waved and Ivan raised a hand in reply. It was a brief greeting. Ivan's business was with the sea and he kept at a distance from the others. They, he knew, could not wait for the trip to end whilst he would have been content to sail for ever chasing an horizon that always ran before him.

His wife and small daughter apart, there were few human beings with whom he felt completely at ease. He preferred a small boat and an empty sea to the company of any man alive and, though this voyage was only beginning, Ivan was already planning his next long sail. In Sumatra in the days of the evacuation he had seen a fishing boat, the *Ko Fuku Maru*, the same with which the *Numbing* and Terry's landing craft had shared the job of rescuing some of the survivors of the Malay campaign. Master sailor that he was, Ivan recognized the strength of the battered boat. She was just the sort of craft he could use to get a group of frogmen into Singapore Harbour in a surprise attack. Once in amongst the anchored shipping the frogmen could wreak tremendous havoc among the enemy ships. It was the kind of buccaneering that appealed to Ivan and during his solitary hours at the wheel of the *Djohanis* he made endless plans. If only he could lay his hands on a craft like the *Maru*, shabby to look at but with powerful engines and sophisticated equipment, it would be easy, he thought, to mount the raid. Although it was 2,400 miles from Western Australia to Singapore it was a long, clean sail and Australia offered obvious advantages as an embarkation point. He realized that his chances of a safe return were slim. Once the explosions started Singapore Harbour would be a trap for any strange craft, however shabby. What the hell, he thought, it's worth a try. His eyes, his only eloquent senses, burned as he made his plans and the hours at the wheel of the *Djohanis* slipped by.

Broome, watching Lyon from the penthouse, thought how like a sparrow the man was with his quick, nervous movements. He was an odd person, unbelievably tough despite his apparent frailness. He had insisted on being at the wheel for far longer than Broome thought endurable, yet he never seemed to tire. T. E. Lawrence must have been much like Ivan, he thought. At the wheel, drinking whisky from the bottle he had been given to help him through the night watches, draped in a gas cape, he looked like a pirate. Broome's eye went back into the penthouse where the off-duty watch were sleeping cramped and huddled for warmth. He realised how tired he was as his own eyelids drooped and his thoughts swam as sleep overcame him. But the man on the wheel, the whisky bottle planted between his feet, felt the strong wind on his back and looked out beyond the night.

While Lyon planned his raid on Singapore the nightly storm had been gathering and soon his face was lashed by wind and the rain drummed on the shiny surface of his gas cape. He wiped the rain from his eyes and glanced at the sails. By now the Sumatras had lost some of their terror and Ivan had the measure of every part and scrap of sail-cloth on the *Djohanis*. He knew how much the prahu could take. Tonight's weather was not violent enough to damage her, he told himself, and he settled down to enjoy the tussle with the storm.

For a while all was well and as the wind died and the rain lessened he could feel the darkness round him like a rug. Beyond him he could hear the crash of the waves and the strong wet slap of water against the hull and his mind examined each noise, catalogued it and put it away. The straining ropes, the creak of shifting timbers, a tin mug that had come loose from the stores rolling to and fro on the deck as the *Djohanis* dipped and pecked. Each separate noise was tabulated and stored in his mind almost without him being aware of it.

Suddenly mental alarm bells started ringing. There was a new noise. Suddenly the crash of the waves had a different sound, harder to catalogue. It was the last sound he had expected to hear so far from land, the defiant lashing of waves on rock.

They were in danger. The sound of the surf was all round him. His eyes narrowed as he peered along the length of the *Djohanis*, helpless to tear away the darkness that shrouded her. But he knew rocks were near. He felt a tightening at the base of his spine and he recognised the instinctive warning. Frantically he put the helm over and the ordered procession of the night noises became a clamour as the *Djohanis* slowly heeled and turned, straining at every timber. The tin mug went spinning across the deck like an alarm bell but the prahu answered to his hands. Lyon had acted just in time. As he looked over the side he saw in the phosphorescence below him the white grin of coral rushing by.

It had been a near thing. A few moments later and the *Djohanis* would have impaled herself on the jagged coral spurs and they would all have been drowned. Lyon wondered by what ancient sense he had been prompted to that sudden change of course. If there were sea gods watching and guarding he blessed them for their intervention.

But this was no time for fancies. The *Djohanis* had scarcely righted herself when once again he heard the waves breaking on coral ahead of him. Again he put the tiller over and watched the coral reef rush almost under the ship. He could hear the surf breaking all about him. They were in a ring of coral, trapped and in terrible danger.

He called to the watch and told them of the peril the *Djohanis* was in.

'I'm sailing her in circles,' he said. 'We've got to get an anchor out at once or we'll be ripped to pieces.'

The men on the watch nodded, scrambled away and seconds later Lyon heard the anchor splashing down. A little later and he felt the pull as the anchor bit into the coral bed below.

It was out of Ivan's hands. Their safety now depended on a thin line of anchor cable. As long as it held they were safe; if it snapped they would be driven on to the coral. He sank to the deck and wrapped his arms round his legs under the gas cape and he rested his head on his knees. Below him the tin mug rolled more slowly now and the *Djohanis* rocked less heavily as she rode at anchor. Soon he was asleep.

Rowley was the first to wake the next morning and he was puzzled when he discovered the ship was not moving. He pulled aside the curtain which hung from the awning of the penthouse.

Outside the bright sun hurt his eyes. He saw Ivan, still sleeping with his head resting on his bent knees, a half-empty bottle of whisky trapped between his feet. Exhausted, thought Rowley as he ducked under the curtain and came out on deck. When he looked about him he saw why.

All around, it seemed in a perfect circle, the waves were breaking over the coral backbone of a ring of reefs and at first Rowley thought he could see no break in their line wide enough to have let the *Djohanis* through to her anchorage. Ivan's feat of helmsmanship that night had been staggering. To have brought the prahu in pitch darkness and in a storm to safety in the very heart of the coral was an amazing achievement and he looked in wonder at the slight figure still huddled at the wheel.

When he woke Ivan waved aside praise. 'We've still got to get out,' he reminded the others when they tried to congratulate him, 'and that's going to be a good deal harder than getting in ever was.'

Anchor raised, the *Djohanis* sailed ponderously round the trap of coral. Again and again they nudged up to what they thought were channels between its banks, only to find inches below the surface gnarled white coral fists that would grind the *Djohanis'* hull into matchwood if they scraped her. They were imprisoned as surely as if they had been rounded up by the Japanese army.

Broome was worried. Their safety from the Japanese aircraft which any moment might be flying over on a morning patrol depended on the *Djohanis* behaving in the way the pilots would expect from native fishing craft. A prahu sailing in circles enmeshed in coral reefs would be sure to raise their suspicions. Something must be done quickly to get the boat on a straight and likely course. In the distance he could see the Plyades light on the tip of a coral finger that stabbed out into the sea in an unbroken line from the Sumatran coast. For all he knew it had been occupied by the Japs and even now they might be under scrutiny from enemy observers.

Ivan beckoned him to the wheel.

'It's a rum go,' he said. 'I daren't run her at the coral. We might just get over but if we do strike I haven't enough control under sail to bring her about before she gets hopelessly damaged. The best thing we can do is to furl the sails and row her very gently where the coral lies deepest and try to edge her over the reef.'

There were groans of dismay when Broome passed on the instruction to the others. The sun was blazing now and without rowlocks the oars, nothing more than heavy rough hewn poles, were awkward and unwieldy.

But they furled the sails and soon they were cursing as the clumsy sweeps slipped and slid along the gunwales of the boat. At last by poling like gondoliers they began to make progress and they felt the jar of the coral beneath them. Once on the coral bed progress became easier as they used its surface to lever the boat forward. Most of the men on the oars had stripped to the waist to make rowing easier and by now the sun was burning into their backs. Their arms ached and their hands were torn and raw against the rough surface of the oars. It was exhausting work and it seemed hours before their oars lost the touch of the coral and they could sense the open sea beneath the hull. They rested on their oars and waited for the order to unfurl the sails. But by now the wind had dropped until there was not a breath from the sea about them and the sweat which ran in rivers from their bodies was unchecked by any breeze on their skins.

'More rowing, I'm afraid,' Broome called. 'That's Plyades out there and this isn't the safest place in the world to hang about.'

The thought of the Japs who might at this moment be watching the *Djohanis* gave the men new energy and with the experience over the reefs behind them the oars were easier to manage, though their weight was still an agony in the broiling sun. Aching muscles became unbearable, all conversation died and when at last they felt the first touch of a returning wind cooling the sweat on their backs, they fell over their oars, worn out. Their rest was brief. Broome sent them scurrying to unfurl the sails before he allowed them to collapse at the foot of the mast, rubbing their muscles.

As they rested they felt the breeze strengthen into a strong wind and the *Djohanis* gathered speed. Soon they were doing five knots and the white pillar of Plyades grew steadily bigger. Their aches forgotten, every man aboard was keyed for the hail, followed by a burst of gunfire, or the sight of a boat putting out from the lighthouse, which would mean they had been spotted by the enemy.

Suddenly the look-out spotted a boat far to port and his hail sent Broome scrambling to the side. The outline of the other boat was diffused in the haze and for a while he could not make her out. He was relieved when Lyon, whose eyes were sharper, called out, 'It's all right, it's another prahu. She's furling her sails. It looks as though she's hit rough weather.'

It was true. Broome could now see the outline of the other fishing boat and she was dipping alarmingly in a mounting sea.

'We'd better do the same,' he cried. 'That squall's going to hit us any minute.'

For the third time that morning Rowley stumped across the deck to the bowsprit and began to swarm up its length to the sail at the tip. The exercise had lost some of its terrors in daylight for by now Rowley had discovered a rudimentary down-hauling apparatus. He had soon inched up the spar and was unfastening the salt-caked shackle preparatory to hauling in the sail. But the salt cut into raw flesh that had been blistered by the oars and he could feel it biting into his hand. It made him clumsy and as he was hauling in the sail it jammed. He struggled to free it and a moment later he heard the sound of ripping canvas as the sail tore down its weakened seam. More sewing he thought as he backed down to the deck in a fury at his own carelessness.

Even under bare poles the *Djohanis* was soon moving at seven knots, the fastest speed of the trip so far. At this rate the danger from the lighthouse would soon be behind them. Douglas was astonished to notice that it was already growing dark. It had taken the best part of the day to pole the boat over the reefs before the wind had risen but the Dutchman's prophecy had been true—no ray of light came from Plyades. If the Japs were there they were not manning the lamps and with every minute the danger of being spotted diminished.

The night was the most uncomfortable they had endured so far and the next morning they awoke to grey and leaden skies which threatened further gales. Unwillingly Rowley joined Douglas and the others as they sat cross-legged round the torn sail. He frowned as Douglas handed him a needle. His dislike of sewing was acute and his discomfort amused the others.

With a start Douglas realised that it had been a month since the fall of Singapore. It seemed an age ago since they had first rowed out to the *Conwy Castle* in the line of junks off the harbour. So many boats, so many adventures. He wondered how long it would be before they would have done with them forever. He longed for the sight of life other than his companions. He wanted to see trees and to feel turf under his feet; to hear bird song and to turn a corner on to new sights instead of this endless monotony of empty seascape. The day before he had seen a flying fish and a school of porpoises dancing on the waves but he wanted buses and droves of people crowding round him.

The leaders were divided. Broome and Jock Campbell, he knew, wanted to land on the next island they reached to take on fresh water. But Lyon, who seemed to draw strength from the empty sea, was opposed to the plan. Bloody Flying Dutchman, thought Douglas, but he could see the force of Lyon's argument. If they missed the North-East monsoon they were lost and they must use every fair wind to get into its path. In April the monsoon would change and its place would be taken by a South-Easter which would drive them into the apex of the Bay of Bengal towards Burma, by now almost certainly in Japanese hands.

It looked to Douglas as though it was going to be a long time before he was able to stretch his legs and his thoughts as he bent over the canvas pushing his needle through the tough sail cloth were dark and unhappy.

At his side Rowley felt little better. Damn all sail needles, he thought, as the point jabbed into his finger. He had never bargained for this sort of job and it did not sit happily with his impatient spirit. He did not share Douglas' longing for an island. The last one had cured him for ever of romantic illusions and he did not much care if he never saw one again. But he would have offered a considerable sum of money for a sewing machine.

10

THE CALL from aft for more sail startled Douglas. The storm was getting worse and he had expected to be told to shorten sail. Any minute he had been expecting to hear the sound of ripping sail and the explosive oath from Rowley which would follow like an echo when he realised that another bout of sewing was inevitable. But he obeyed the orders from the helmsman and struggled with the canvas in the driving rain.

The sea leapt under the *Djohanis* as she tossed on the biggest of the waves and burrowed her way through the walls of spray. It was almost impossible to stand upright on deck and he was repeatedly thrown against the mast as he struggled with the halyards.

No sooner had the extra sail been crammed on than the gale blew with fresh force, biting into the cloths and spars. There was a sound of breaking wood—the mizzen halyard had given way and the boom crashed against one of the stays, smashing it and leaving the sail flapping in the storm.

Slipping and crawling, fighting to stay upright, all hands rushed to bring in the useless canvas. 'For God's sake, be careful,' shouted Rowley. 'We don't want to be sewing again.'

They were able to haul in the sail without tearing it but they had scarcely recovered from their struggle when the Doc shouted a warning.

'The water kegs are going.'

The violence of the storm had thrown the kegs repeatedly against the ropes that lashed them to the deck and each frantic lurch had put increased pressure on the knots that secured them. A final mighty heave and the knots burst, releasing the drums to slide crazily about the deck.

The gale howled and the rain knocked the breath from their bodies as they inched towards the drums of water. But they were too late. Even as they reached them one of the drums crashed against the gunwale and its contents gushed out to mingle with the house-high waves that thundered into the prahu. They worked like demons but by the time they were able to secure the drums over half of their precious water supply had gone.

Exhausted, the men slid and crawled down the deck until they could find something to cling to, to save them from being swept against the gunwales or over the side.

The loss of water, they knew, was the worst disaster that could have overtaken them. With little food they might have carried on but without water under the baking sun in the middle of the Indian Ocean they were lost. They slumped in sickened despair.

The Doc spoke first. Over the wind and the crashing of the waves his voice was steady and reassuring.

'At least when we get out to sea we will be free of these awful land storms,' he told them. The thought cheered the others, as he had intended, and one by one they answered him with smiles. It was not much of a bright side but it was worth looking on.

Lyon was magnificent at the helm and once again, when daylight broke on 16 March, they found themselves in the centre of a nest of coral islands. The Doc looked around him in disbelief. He could not see how the *Djohanis* had escaped being pitched on to the coral which broke through the seas about them.

'It must be providence,' he said. 'Someone's on our side.'

Lt Brian Passmore aboard the *nglo-Canadian*.

9. Doc Davies washing his 'smalls' aboard the *Anglo-Canadian*.

10. The moment of rescue by the *Anglo-Canadian* was the most dangerous of the voyage. The signal the army officers ran up to attract the attention of the merchantman read 'Am preparing to attack'.

11. & 12. Aboard the *Anglo-Canadian* – *above* Spanton and Waller; *below* Doc Davies and Jock Campbell.

It was a dubious providence. Storm followed storm and the *Djohanis* fled from the turbulence under bare poles chased by the angry winds: the lightning ripped at the sky to the heavy applause of thunder.

The men's faith in the *Djohanis* was growing for all the violence of the storms. They were finding their sea legs, too, and the pitching of the boat bothered them less by the hour. Now the worst moments came when the wind dropped and the *Djohanis* was left rolling in the heavy seas unable to continue under way.

Shortly before dawn on 17 March, another great storm hit the little ship with deafening thunder-claps. The rain was more than welcome. They searched for any container they could find to collect the water. Jock Campbell knew that they would soon be sailing beyond the range of these coastal downpours and he was anxious to replenish his stores while the opportunity still offered. Everyone turned out to catch water and the sails were lowered and laid over the hatch with a man at each corner. As the canvas filled with water they folded the sail and ran its contents into two buckets from which they refilled the empty casks.

Douglas was soon surrounded by an array of mugs, basins and frying pans and he used a gas cape to channel the rain into them. In this way they caught, by the Doc's reckoning, at least twenty gallons of water and the supply tanks were almost full again.

For Rowley the worst part of the morning was the water spouts that skimmed over the surface of the sea. At one time he counted no less than seven of the great elephants' trunks of water in the dying storms, dancing along the sea, any one of which, if it had struck the ship, would have been powerful enough to strip the sails and the rigging.

The calm that followed was a holiday for them all. With the pleasant taste of the rain on their tongues the men lay about the deck talking and telling stories. Gorham wore a vast panama hat made from palm leaves and Spanton searched through the stores until he found sufficient thin cord to make a fishing line. He fashioned a hook from a piece of steel wire and, settling himself at the stern, he whistled as the cord dropped into the water behind the boat.

The others watched idly as Spanton re-cast his line.

'Your only chance is to hit one on the head with that great hook,' Rowley, the expert, told him kindly. 'You may stun it.'

Stanton ignored him as he felt a tug on his line. 'I've got one, I've got one,' he shouted excitedly as the line went tight. 'It's a bloody monster. I can hardly hold it.'

The fish was a fighter. Encumbered by the advice of his companions Spanton gave line as sparingly as possible until he was left with only the last few inches to grip in his hands. His imperturbability had gone. His eyes were blazing with excitement, and the men watched, not daring to speak. But a moment later the line broke. Spanton felt the sudden deadness of the cord. He looked around him at the crestfallen faces of his companions and his own expression was almost comic in its grief.

Opportunities for sport on the *Djohanis* were limited and watching Spanton had awakened the hunting instinct in them all. A fly hunt was a modest substitute but it had some of the thrills of the chase and they organized a safari. Their motives were not wholly sporting. There had been a plague of flies on the *Djohanis*. During the storms the insects had found shelter in any crack in the wood, palm frond or coil of canvas that offered protection from the weather. But the warm sun had wakened them and each man was told off to kill ten flies a day. The killing went on until the last fly was killed and thrown overboard.

Cockroaches were a more serious problem. The Doc had been puzzled to notice that the men were losing patches of hair. At first he was inclined to attribute the loss to the monotony of the diet and the lack of vitamins. The discovery that the men's hair was being eaten by cockroaches which grazed on their heads as they slept brought shudders to even the most hardened of the men on the ship. Lind, half asleep, was the first to discover their unwelcome guests. He felt faint, almost indiscernible tugs on his back hair. Absently he brushed at his head, and his hand came into contact with the moist scaliness of an insect. It brought him to his feet with a howl that awakened the sleepers round him. Hotly he returned their growled complaints.

'D'you want me to lie there and be eaten alive?' he demanded.

When he told the others about the cockroach they passed an uneasy night waiting for the return of the loathsome insects. At dawn they searched for the holes in which the cockroaches were lying up but there were too many hiding places in the ship, especially in the inaccessible bilges, so the cockroaches stayed to plague them.

The *Djohanis* made her best speed on 18 March. In twenty-four hours she sailed 102 miles before a strong but changeable breeze. Unfortunately it brought them no nearer their destination. The North wind pushed them too far to the South-West and they prayed in vain that the North-East monsoon would strengthen and blow from its proper quarter again.

The meetings of the Fo'c'sle Club were the centre of the ship's life. With Passmore accompanying them on a banjo, they sang, as their mood varied, hymns and as many Rugby changing room songs as they could remember. At the earlier meetings food had been the major topic in the club discussions and their favourite reading at this time was the cookery section in the dog-eared copies of 'Esquire' that were passed from hand to hand. One which was a particular favourite of Rowley's described in detail how to stuff a turkey with alternate layers of oysters and toast. He resolved if ever they did reach Ceylon to order the largest turkey he could buy and stuff it with barrels of oysters on rafts of hot buttered toast.

The beauties in the pin-up section of the magazine would no doubt have been furious if they had known that for eighteen of the magazine's most devoted readers they thrusted and pouted in vain. They preferred the Seager's advertisement which showed gin in polished glasses that held ice and the carnival bubbles of tonic water. At length so acute did the torture become to men rationed to an army mug of water a day that gastronomy, by general agreement, was banished as a topic.

Meals on the *Djohanis* were spartan. At 7 am Jock Campbell handed out breakfast which consisted of three liberally buttered biscuits, two army and one Marie, and a third of a cup of coffee.

Lunch at midday for 18 men consisted of three tins of salmon or bully beef, two tins of carrots and one of potatoes, varied every third day with a tin of tomatoes. Every fifth day there was a change of menu to fried rice mixed with salmon or bully beef, or boiled rice with sugar and condensed milk added. The amount of fresh water needed to soak it made it impossible to serve rice more often and rice soaked in sea water did little to ease their thirst. Every third or fourth day three tins of pears or mixed fruits were shared out. Two biscuits with butter or margarine and a third of a mug of tea completed the meal. Supper varied from lunch hardly at all. If the men had been given salmon for lunch they got bully for supper and vice-versa. In times of stress an extra third of a pint of water was distributed which they could draw at any time between supper and breakfast. Early in the voyage the diet had been supplemented by fresh limes and bananas they had bought on their island shopping trip but these were soon exhausted.

When storms and the trials of shipboard life threatened to crush their spirits each man was given afternoon tea at 3 pm. It consisted of a small piece of tinned cherry cake and a third of a pint of tea. With the exception of the extra ration, all water was given as tea or coffee because it was safer to do so and because the thirst-quenching properties of the brews were greater than that of water alone.

From his vantage point on the fo'c'sle the Doc kept an anxious watch on the health of his companions and he made careful notes in the diary he was keeping of the trip.
He wrote:

> It is extremely interesting to be in a position to follow the general health of the men. Almost all have been through trying conditions during the month prior to starting the journey and could hardly be described as being in good health. The first ten days of fighting continual squalls before getting 'sea legs' had put an extra strain on physique in general.

Like a country doctor in the quiet of his surgery the Doctor went on with his notes:

> It is curious to notice how the mental outlook varies with changes of the wind, the vital factor in the trip. Whenever the wind is in the wrong quarter or calm prevails, everyone's spirits are at a low ebb but when it changes to North-East no matter how hard it blows everyone becomes more cheerful. I have taken general precautions against sunburn by warning everybody immediately of the dangers of exposure and the importance of only gradually increasing the areas of flesh exposed in order to prevent acute sunburn. Happily these instructions have been strictly complied with and although everybody is now very sunburnt no-one has required more than a mild application of ointments.
>
> Sea-sickness has caused very little trouble and everybody has been able to carry on working even in the worst seas. We have three hundred tablets of Celin (Vitamin C) which we began taking after all our fresh fruit had gone and after a suitable interval has elapsed I shall give the men two tablets a day as long as stocks last. In addition we have three bottles of lime juice which will give an additional source of vitamins when the tablets are gone.
>
> Sepsis is our main worry. It is impossible to have a good wash in sea water and although everyone bathes two or

three times daily they cannot work up a lather in the salt water. Diarrhoea or constipation have been noticeable features during the first days, no doubt due to the change of food and short rations.

Everyone is going about either bare-legged or bare-footed and it is interesting to notice how hard the sole of a foot can become in a short time.

In his General Log he wrote:

> 20 March The wind still blowing in the wrong direction, chiefly W.S.W. Japanese over twice, once at breakfast and once at lunch. Their reconnaissance seems fairly good. Dead calm from lunch-time onwards. Everybody, save the helmsman, lies inside the penthouse in the afternoon. Though very hot it is better than being in the open. Some sleep and some read.
> 21 March Still dead calm. Japanese again over twice. General spirits low owing to lack of progress. The evening sessions of the Fo'c'sle Club, however, are very cheerful.
> 22 March A slight wind with a suggestion of N.E. about it. Japanese over twice again.
> 23 March The wind is stronger. Japanese over only once. Later a storm blew up which we ran before. Unfortunately we were slow in getting the mainsail down which tore. The sails are causing much worry and annoyance. They are so thin that the stars are visible through them and in raising and lowering them they are continually catching on something and tearing. Gorham has started a party on making a new storm sail and mizzen.
> 24 March No Japanese planes over today which has put up general morale immensely. It is hoped that we are now on our way and out of range.

Douglas Fraser noted on the same day in his pocket diary:

> We have done well since yesterday although the wind takes us too far South off our course. We are now 784 miles

from Colombo. We tried making up a bit of North but are now going strong on a West by South course whereas we want W.N.W. I suppose the wind will change soon.

The next day he wrote:

> I am getting slack at writing this but I think everyone is feeling slack. We have had two days of calm and have made pretty well no headway which makes it very hot and discouraging. No one minds about food of which we really have plenty if we are careful, but we are frightened of running out of water. We seem to have gallons of it but if this surfeit of calms and contrary winds continues we must be very careful. Jock Campbell intimated that if things do not improve tomorrow we shall have to reduce the water ration and do away with the drink we get at night. At the moment we get a pint of water a day in tea or coffee. Everyone LIVES for the tea and coffee.
>
> A swallow which landed on the rigging two days ago is still with us and quite tame. It takes water thirstily when given it.
>
> We are making another sail for the mizzen to use in storms so that we can steer a course in dirty weather instead of careering hopelessly before the wind. 18.00 to 20.00 is very pleasant on the foredeck in the cool of the evening. It is 13.15 hours and here is hoping for a decent breeze in the right direction by this evening or else the extra water ration is discontinued.

But the dead calm continued for another three days until the evening of the 28th and the extra water ration was cut off.

The *Djohanis* wallowed on the flat sea. The bilges began to smell and the sun beat down mercilessly. Bored by the inactivity Jock Campbell decided to try out the spare battery for the wireless set. Radio time was hoarded more carefully even than the water. The wireless gave them a time check without which accurate navigation would have been impossible. Testing the spare battery would mean playing the radio for a little while and Jock thought it would provide a welcome diversion. He lifted the spare battery from its place amongst the stores and handed it over to Gorham, the navigator. Happily it had escaped damage in the bad weather and the others gathered round him as he wound the wires round the terminals of the battery.

It was nearly time for the news and everyone was anxious to know the progress of the war. Mostly they feared an invasion of Burma and the overrunning of Ceylon by victorious Japanese armies. To have sailed so far only to fall once again into the hands of the Japanese would have been unbearable.

Gorham reached for the switch to turn on the wireless. It was silent. The spare battery was a dud and only the slap of the flat sea on the ship's sides could be heard on deck. Gorham sent the station finding arm racing across the dial searching for a sign of life in any language but it was no use. The battery was dead. He swore as he disconnected it and, carrying it to the side, hurled it as far as he could into the sea. It gave him a brief and savage satisfaction to watch it sink.

The dud battery was a terrible blow. They had only the waning power of the other one now and they would only be able to use it for, at most, a minute a day. If their calculations went wrong and they missed the daily time check it would be twelve hours before they could correct their navigation. They were in a mess and they knew it. In the hours that followed resentments flared.

The good companionship of a favourable wind was fading and there was a sharp edge to their voices when they spoke. Rowley found himself watching resentfully the way Douglas hovered round the food as it was being dished out and felt sudden spasms of unreasonable anger. Douglas whose appetite was the heartiest of any of them was suffering agonies of hunger. The mood affected even the imperturbable Doc. Spanton, he thought impatiently, seemed to have requisitioned the canoe for himself, whilst Spanton lay in a world of his own, hardly speaking.

Even the sighting of an aircraft brought hostility. Waller, forgetting the orders to stay under cover, ran to the side, shouting,

'My God, it's a Flying Fortress,' and everyone rushed to join him. Douglas shouted at them not to go outside but they ignored him. All planes in these waters should be considered to be hostile, he reckoned, but consoled himself with the view that it was probably ten miles away and the *Djohanis* would show only as a speck in the ocean.

The swallow brought to the *Djohanis* more than it knew. It flew over the little ship and landed, exhausted, on one of the spars. Summing up the humans below as harmless it fluttered down first on to the atap roof and finally into the penthouse itself. The men watched it, hardly daring to breathe in case they frightened it away. It dominated the interest of everyone in the cabin as it hopped about examining them and their possessions. Someone offered it a crumb and the bird ate it greedily. Immediately everyone began searching for crumbs for the visitor. Holly picked it up gently and stroked its head. The swallow lay in his hand, its bright eyes watching him. The Doc brought water in a bottle cap and the bird buried its beak in the water and began to drink. The tensions of the becalmed days were eased, and that night the Fo'c'sle club had one of its merriest meetings. On the perch it had chosen in the atap roof the swallow slept soundly through their singing.

The next day the heat was unbearable and the men sat in listless groups, their energy drained. Those who had towels dipped them in the sea and wrapped them round their shoulders, their skins soaking in the water. It brought small relief for the sun dried the towels out almost at once and the process had to be repeated.

Douglas was restless. He was too hot even to talk. His diary was written up to date, lunch seemed hours ago and supper too far ahead to bear thinking of. He chafed at his inactivity.

'I'm going for a swim,' he said and before anyone had time

to do anything more than express astonishment he had stripped off his ragged shorts and disappeared in a graceful dive over the side. For five minutes in the freedom of the Indian Ocean he forgot about wars and escapes and short rations and cockroaches. The water was cool and invigorating, although the salt bit into his sun-burnt back. He swam slowly back to the ship and climbed over the side.

Gorham looked at him with approval. 'That is a hell of a good idea,' he said. Broome was standing at the stern of the *Djohanis* looking behind them.

'Perhaps not,' he suggested, pointing out to sea. They followed the line of his finger to the place where, a moment before, Douglas had been swimming. A curved fin broke the surface. Douglas watched in horror. Its outline broken and hazy under the water, the shark was all of eight feet long.

Broome turned, 'I think that will be the last swimming party of the trip,' he said.

The men were silent. It was unpleasant to think of their fate if the *Djohanis* sank in a storm or under the guns of a Japanese plane.

That night the swallow flew away.

II

THE ATTACK began as the men were preparing breakfast in the shade of the penthouse. At first they paid no attention to the plane, a small silver crucifix in the sky above their heads. Japanese reconnaissance flights were a daily event and after the first days of the voyage they had ignored them. But the cry from Lind who was on lookout sent every head swivelling to the sky.

'It's spotted us,' he shouted, his voice shrill. 'It's circling. My God it's going to attack.'

They had rehearsed their drill many times. It had been agreed that Jamal and Soon would make themselves as conspicuous as possible in the hope that they would be mistaken for Malays on a fishing trip. As the plane dived the two coloured men took up their places on the stern while the white men ran for cover.

Inside the penthouse Rowley could see the bomber through the atap roof. It was coming at them so fast it seemed to be falling out of the sky. As he watched Soon and Jamal abandoned their perch and dived for cover and he heard the thud of bullets as they hit the sides of the prahu. Rowley dived on to the mattress which covered the floor of the penthouse. He knew that the greatest danger would be from splinters and ricochets from the stones which were used as rudimentary ballast in the bilges of the *Djohanis*. The mattress would be some sort of protection he thought, as he spread-eagled himself across its surface. But quick as Rowley had been, the Doc reached the mattress almost at the same moment as he did, burrowing desperately to get beneath it out of the way of the bullets that whistled through the atap over their heads.

The mattress heaved as the two men struggled for possession.

'For God's sake get under, man,' roared the Doctor.

'Find your own mattress,' Rowley roared back. 'Can't you see this one is taken?'

As they argued Douglas looked desperately about him. The only protection he could see were the cases of stores and he started piling them against the walls of the penthouse. The ship's biscuits were thick enough to stop any bullet but he wondered what their fate would be if the plane dropped a bomb. Uncomfortably he thought of the sharks. At his feet the battle for the mattress raged. Red with the heat and the effort the Doc had managed to burrow almost to the centre rolling Rowley to the far edge where he sat, pink with asperity.

'I suppose you realize,' he said, raising his voice over the roar of the bomber as it dived again 'that your feet are sticking out.'

The Doc's reply was muffled under the heavy covering but he drew his legs in sharply and the mattress humped under his bulk sending Rowley crashing against the atap. As he scrambled up he heard the sound of the bomber's engines getting fainter. It was gaining height. Plainly the attack had been an act of mischief by a bored pilot and tail gunner. He turned to the mattress and addressed the hump that covered the anguished Doctor.

'You may care to know,' he said with icy relish, 'that by now the plane is probably five miles away.'

There was a brief silence. Then the Doc emerged slowly from under the mattress. Ruffled but with measured dignity he glared at Rowley, 'It's not a doctor you need, my boy, it's a bloody psychiatrist. In all my life...'

But the sight of the doctor, his face smudged with dust and crimson with exertion was too much for the others and the rest of his remarks were drowned in their laughter. He glared about him indignantly but soon he too was grinning. The raid was over and they were safe. Outside he could hear the sounds of a growing wind.

'It's a North-Easter,' shouted Gorham. 'We've got it. The Monsoon again.'

The attack was forgotten in the excitement which followed as the others scrambled out on to the deck where Gorham was standing with his arms outstretched.

'Oh you lovely, lovely wind,' he cried.

For days the North-Easter had teased them, gathering strength and then dying away to leave them once again becalmed. Now it struck them with force and the *Djohanis* went scuttling before it. In high spirits the men went round inspecting the damage from the raid. Five bursts of machine-gun fire had struck the ship but apart from broken crockery there was no serious harm done. But the attack had shown them how quickly danger could strike and they set about making the ship as bullet proof as circumstances allowed. Mattresses were laid on the forward and after platforms of the penthouse, after Rowley had explained to the Doc his theories about stone splinters, and cases of bully beef and carrots were stacked amidships against the ship's sides as protection against machine-gun attack. As a final precaution the Carley floats were unshipped and stowed where they could easily be reached in the event of the *Djohanis* being holed.

The next morning the men waited uneasily for the sound of engines. Breakfast was a scrappy meal and the men chewed absent-mindedly, the edge of their hunger blunted by the thought of what the morning might bring. Once Soon dropped a pan and everyone jumped but the morning wore on and no plane appeared. The men began to go about their work and the atmosphere became calmer.

Once again it was Gorham whose news brought them clustering to the case on which he had spread his scrappy charts. They had passed the half-way mark and the coast of Ceylon was only 496 miles away he told them. Better, they were firmly in the grip of the North-Easter, so it would only be a matter of days before they saw the coastline. Everyone was jubilant and Campbell celebrated the news by giving every man an extra pint of water with his rations.

In their new-found high spirits they looked about for ways of increasing the speed of the *Djohanis*. Lashed into the shrouds with a hole cut in its floor was a coffin-like wooden construction which served both as bathroom and lavatory. In its former role the men climbed into it from a step ladder on the deck and pulled buckets of sea water up through the hole in the floor to sluice themselves. To use it as a lavatory they squatted over the hole in the floor.

Though Brooke, the Royal Naval man, was punctilious in his morning visits, for most of the crew two or even three days would pass before they found it necessary to climb into the shrouds. In heavy seas the latrine hit the waves when the *Djohanis* rolled. Its resistance and weight threw her off balance and they decided it must go. Despite Brooke's protests it was cut from the rigging and he watched unhappily as the thunderbox floated away.

When next the others looked at him Brooke was splicing and plaiting ends of rope into a complicated harness and when it was ready he climbed out into the shrouds to fix it in place where the thunderbox had been. As the others watched he contorted himself into the harness so that he could lean out over the ocean. Even in rough seas when the water came up to one's arm pits a man could hang there in safety. 'It looks like a rupture appliance,' said the Doc and Brooke's Apparatus, in deference to a well-known rupture appliance of the day, it became for the rest of the voyage.

On 1 April the men collected 30 gallons of rain water and as a reward Jock gave each man two extra cigarettes and a Marie biscuit. By now not even the distant sight of an aircraft or Douglas's warnings could dampen their spirits.

Every natural force seemed to be working for them. When the wind dropped, currents carried them fifty miles nearer to their objective in two days. Their greatest worry was their daily time check. The radio had used up the last of the battery and there was no way in which they could plot a course.

Under her makeshift sails the *Djohanis* scudded over the seas but the rough weather and multiple storms through which she fought meant hard work for her crew. Once Broome had to be lugged aloft in an improvised bosun's chair to the top of the mainmast when the throat stuck. As he watched him climb Douglas noticed that the pendulum which Ivan Lyon had fixed to the mast was swinging far beyond the safety line and it seemed that the force of the wind must rip Broome from the soaked and slippery wood. Douglas could see him shaking his head in the blinding spray. Three times he slipped and the others saw the blood run where the mast had rubbed the skin from his legs. Somehow he managed to retain his grip and after what seemed an age he was stretching out into the shrouds to release the sail which fell in a wet heap on the deck.

Once again embryo water spouts appeared to plague them. It was as though a school of whales were playing beneath the surface, taunting the little boat with playful rushes. But they were able to collect a further ten gallons of rain water and Jock estimated that by now they had enough water to last them through the trip.

The new storm rigging was an unqualified success and a blustering wind continued to blow them due West before it. Under a butterfly spread of canvas they made 81 miles in 24 hours. Ceylon was getting nearer by the hour. By Gorham's latest estimate they had only 231 miles to go.

Gorham and Passmore had been working together on the

radio set and had managed to get the beginning of the news broadcast. The war news was depressing but at least it was a contact with the world. Once again the duty watch huddled round the set straining to hear every word they could catch amongst the atmospherics that distorted the announcer's voice.

They had missed the Greenwich time signal which preceded the news but Gorham was able to calculate the probable time from the bulletin. He glanced at the watch on his wrist to check its accuracy. It was crucial. On this depended all the calculations which were necessary to bring the *Djohanis* safely across the ocean. What he saw stunned him. His watch was slow and the whole fabric of his calculations was torn asunder. After a hasty recalculation he realized that they had 109 miles further to go than he had estimated. He went over his figures again and again, but they were unalterable. His voice was broken when he announced his error. There had been days on the trip when they had done less than fifteen miles. Suppose they hit another period of calm? It could put an extra ten days or more on their journey. The thought sent their spirits tumbling as the implications of the miscalculation hit them.

The past twenty-four hours of storms had meant working almost continuously on the sails and they were all exhausted. What if the wind changed to a South-Wester and they were once again faced with the danger of being blown towards the coast of Burma? Sensing their despair Jock Campbell opened one of the remaining bottles of whisky and that afternoon tea and cherry cake was served.

In the world about them great events were shaping. Warned that Japan was planning a large-scale invasion of Ceylon Admiral Somerville had concentrated his fleet to the south to do battle. On 4 April a Catalina flying-boat had sighted a Japanese fleet in the Bay of Bengal, but it was shot down before it could signal back the fleet's strength. The next day Colombo came under attack from 80 Japanese dive

13. Shaved and spruce the escapees pose with the officers of the *Anglo-Canadian*.

14. The shelling of the *Sederhana Djohanis*. The Captain of the ship which picked up the escapees feared that, left to drift, the crewless prahau would be a menace to shipping.

15. Sails shot away and holed, the *Djohanis* defies the guns of the *Anglo-Canadian*.

16. The *Djohanis* brought her crew 1,659 miles across the Indian Ocean in 36 days, 13 hours and 31 minutes. Now from the deck of the *Anglo-Canadian* the men who sailed in her watch the prahau disappear over the horizon.

bombers. The enemy lost 21 planes but 19 British fighters and 6 Swordfish Fleet Air Arm planes were shot down and the destroyer *Tenedos* and the merchant cruiser *Hector* were sunk at their moorings in the attack which lasted for 90 minutes. The same day the *Dorsetshire* and the *Cornwall* were attacked and sunk by Japanese dive bombers. A total of 29 officers and 295 men died and the 1,122 survivors were rescued after 36 hours in the water in open boats.

On 9 April, 54 Japanese bombers attacked Trincomalee and damaged the dockyard, workshops and the airfield. 15 enemy planes were shot down for the loss of 11 British planes but half the remaining bomber force which had been sent out to attack the Japanese aircraft carriers were also shot down. That day the aircraft carrier *Hermes* and the destroyer *Vampire* were sunk.

The Japanese Naval forces were commanded by the same Admiral Nagumo who had launched the attack on Pearl Harbour. His force in the Indian Ocean consisted of 5 aircraft carriers and 4 fast battleships, besides cruisers, destroyers and their accompanying tankers. A second Japanese task force consisting of a light carrier and 6 heavy cruisers steamed unopposed into the Bay of Bengal to attack merchant shipping. In all 116,000 tons of shipping were lost.

And into this holocaust the *Djohanis* was unwittingly sailing with its crew of weary and despondent men. Mercifully the flashes they saw in the distance and the rumbling of the naval guns meant only one thing to them. Another storm was on the way and they prayed the wind would blow them in the right direction.

The Doc's worries were more immediate. He noticed that some of the men were becoming septic.

In his diary he wrote:

> Sepsis is the main cause of my worries. It is impossible to have a good wash in sea water and although everyone washes two or three times daily it is impossible to work up

a lather. This is probably the chief cause of the sepsis. The lesions are either fulminating ulcers resulting from trauma or a generalised eruption of vesicles and pustules usually in the axillae, belt areas, groin and buttocks. Three cases of fulminating ulcers occurred with spreading lymphangitis and adenitis but they were all successfully treated with purgation, sea water fomentations every four hours and M. and B. 693 QDS. The vesicles and pustules which appear to be of the nature of a bulbous impetigo or tropical pemphigus are far more difficult to deal with and as the journey nears what we hope is its end they are becoming more generalised throughout the party. Many different treatments have been tried, swabbing with eau-de-cologne, dettols, M. and B. 693, talcum powder and germolene but the best appeared to be that of swabbing with eau-de-cologne, leaving to dry and applying talcum powder twice daily. I feel that a stock of cod liver oil would benefit them in their present condition.

The fact that only one case of tinea interdigitalis has occurred has been an excellent lesson in the importance of aeration of the feet. Almost everyone has lost a considerable amount of weight, most of which was superfluous and could be spared and apart from somewhat hollow cheeks and sunken eyes due to partial dehydration and lack of sleep, everyone is looking fairly healthy.

The long voyage went on. In twenty-four hours of battering by storms and squalls the *Djohanis* sailed exactly seven miles. The bantering mood in which the trip had started was gone now and when they came off duty the men wanted only to crawl under the atap roof to shelter from the sun. The only gaiety came during the evening meetings of the Fo'c'sle club and sometimes even this brief relaxation was wrapped in gloom.

Gorham's navigational error, although hardly his fault, had badly bruised their morale and now they were less ready to take his estimate of the distance they had still to sail. It was as well that they did not know that in the Indian Ocean around them infinitely better found ships than theirs were being sunk out of hand by the superior forces of the Japanese Navy.

As dawn heralded the end of his watch, Douglas was leaning over the side of the boat staring vacantly into the water below. Suddenly out of the corner of his eye he caught the quick golden flash of a small body. He thought it was a fish and he leaned further out over the side. But it wasn't a fish; it was metal. The copper which lined the outside of the hull of the *Djohanis* was peeling away. Slowly the little craft was disintegrating. The massive buffeting she had taken in the last twenty-nine days was beginning to take its toll. Douglas's mind went back to the shark.

12

DOUGLAS HURRIED across to where Rowley was sleeping and his whisper was urgent.
'Rowley, wake up. For God's sake wake up.'
Rowley shook his head angrily.
'What the hell's the matter?' he growled.
Anxiously Douglas told him about the copper.
'What are we going to do? Shall we tell the others?'
Rowley thought for a moment.
'I think we'll have to,' he said. 'There's nothing to be gained by keeping it to ourselves. It's the sort of thing it is better to know.'
They told the others that morning after breakfast and the news brought low whistles of dismay.
'That's it,' said Jock Campbell. Holly said nothing but he stroked the white bristles on his chin and the Doc looked quietly from one man to another. Rowley searched the faces round him as Douglas told his story. It was the older men who took the news most calmly. The younger ones rushed to the side to confirm Douglas's story, while the older ones sat over their plates in silence.
Broome broke the silence.
'There's no immediate danger, of course, but it cuts our safety margin. We can't afford any major navigational errors.'

He looked up quickly at Gorham's muttered protest.

'I'm not blaming you, Garth. You've put up a bloody good show to get us this far but every mile we go off course now reduces our chance of reaching land.'

His helplessness infuriated Rowley. Re-sheathing or even repairing the hull was a major repair job for which they had neither the ability nor the tools.

'Perhaps we'll be picked up soon,' said Lind hopefully. 'A Catalina. Perhaps a lovely great flying boat will come out of the sky and spot us. Just think of it. Flying back to Ceylon. A couple of hours and we'd all be sitting in arm-chairs with whacking great gin and tonics. And a long, long bath. Think of a bath...'

His voice trailed away and for a while he sat in silence, but Gorham soon jerked him back into reality.

'Think of those bloody sharks,' he said. 'There's only one bath we're due for and I, for one, want to put it off as long as I can.'

He looked out over the side of the *Djohanis* and the others shuddered as they followed his gaze. Jock Campbell felt the depression growing. He got to his feet and tried to sound cheerful.

'No gin, I'm afraid,' he said. 'But I've got something of the same colour. What about a mug of water?'

For Jock to break the strict régime of rationing was an unheard of thing and they brightened up at the thought of an extra share. They watched as he drew off mugs of water from the nearest keg and their eyes followed him thirstily as he came back with their rations. Their mouths were dry as sandpaper and already the sun was starting rivers of sweat down their bodies. Eagerly Rowley reached for a mug, wiping the salt from his lips so that nothing should mar the taste of this unexpected treat. Both hands round the mug he raised it to his lips. He wished he had a gallon of it. A moment later he had spat out the water and jumping to his feet he banged the mug down violently. His face was screwed up in disgust.

'The bloody stuff's gone bad,' he roared.

In disbelief the others drank from their mugs but soon they too were spitting out the water and shuddering from the bad-egg taste it left in their mouths. It was undrinkable even to men driven to the very edge of thirst. This was a disaster more immediate than the slow peeling of the copper for without water they were lost and they watched in silence as Jock hurriedly broached the other cask.

'It could be worse,' he announced. 'Only one keg has gone bad. It must have been something in the wood.'

But he knew that one bad keg was enough to put their survival in peril and there was no lightness left in him as he rejoined the silent group as they sat in the shade of the penthouse. They were all plunged in gloom so deep it seemed they could never surface and they listened dully to the monotonous slap of the sail and the dull thud of the water against the hull. The rising smell from the bilges filled their throats and not even the sudden arrival of the wind for which they had waited so long could raise their spirits. They moved about their tasks listlessly as the caprice of the wind made sudden changes of sail necessary, coming at them in turn from every quarter of the sky. No one complained, few even cursed as they worked, wrapped in the black homespun of their thoughts.

The Doc had been looking into the sky. Suddenly he stiffened and pointed.

'Look,' he cried. 'Up there. Can you see what I see?'

Aware of the ever-present menace of Jap bombers the men on the deck looked up to follow his pointing finger. Above them in formation and flying with the lazy skill of instinct was a flock of birds. The Doc was overjoyed.

'Surely that means we can't be too far from land?' he asked.

The birds brought new hope and that evening the Fo'c'sle club had one of its most successful meetings with Rowley airing his voice on the failings of the army in Singapore and the iniquities of the racing authorities in Malaya. The Club was still inclined to distrust Gorham's estimate of their position. The monsoon seemed to be changing and they thought they were more likely to be blown to Madras than to Ceylon. They chafed at the useless radio. More than anything they wanted to hear news of the world which was fighting for its life over the horizon and they wondered why it was that neither the Royal Navy nor the R.A.F. had crossed their path.

'In my opinion,' said Rowley crossly, 'they are losing a good deal of face.'

His opinion was shared by the Club.

Earlier that day the mainsail had torn across its whole length. Ivan had climbed to the top of the mizzen mast and tried to free it from a snag in which it was caught but he only succeeded in ripping it. The men had never had a tear as large as this one to repair and they looked at it blankly. Jock Campbell sized up their feelings and took the sail across his knees.

'Don't worry; leave it to me,' he said.

As the others watched he picked away the stitches to take out the centre panel of the sail. By dusk he had finished and the watch called their congratulations as they hauled the now smaller but stronger mizzen sail up the mast. They were only just in time. As the sail was raised the wind steadied and shifted firmly to the north-east. The sky cleared and the *Djohanis* was once again under way. The good wind held all night and in the morning when the off-duty watch wakened they learned of the progress the *Djohanis* had made whilst they slept and scrambled out on deck to confirm the report of their companions. The sea was alive with the wind. The sky was clear and the occasional clouds which crossed it were like a far shore, majestic and inviolate.

Ivan ordered every inch of canvas to be hoisted and now as they ran before the wind, the tiller leapt in his hand, a living thing. Ivan never tired. He was delighted when, the next morning, a storm broke on the starboard quarter and the *Djohanis* began what proved to be the best run of the trip.

'This is glorious,' said the Doc and Douglas answered excitedly, 'She's going like a train.'

A moment later Doc gripped Douglas by the arm. 'We're in a tide race,' he said.

'We can't be. According to Gorham's calculations we've still got 252 miles to go. He can't be that far out, surely?'

But the Doc was firm. 'It's a tide race, I tell you. Look.' And he pointed to the sea ahead of them. Sure enough, Douglas could feel the pull of the current plucking at the keel of the *Djohanis*. When they called to the others no one could account for the tide race, although unquestionably that was what it was and excited discussion brought lunch-time quickly.

Lunch was a disappointment. Jock Campbell had seen the spirits of the men rise before only to be dashed when the wind dropped. It was true that the monsoon seemed set and in such strength that it was unlikely that it would desert them for at least some time. Unlikely, he thought, but not impossible and he knew that if the monsoon did die the men's present high spirits would die with it. When that happened the extra rations would be needed. Besides, their rations were only sufficient now so long as they made a good daily average time. Even two days becalmed on a dead sea would be enough to wreck his carefully laid programme. He decided to reduce the size of the portions. So lunch that day for the eighteen consisted of three tins of salmon, two of beans, two biscuits and a third of a pint of water.

'It's incredible,' the Doc thought. 'No complaints.'

He recalled his earlier observations of the way morale rose and fell with the wind. The monsoon was a curious medicine but it never failed to improve his patients.

Unfortunately trouble followed the *Djohanis* as surely as the friendly wind. That afternoon they heard the sound of an aeroplane. By Gorham's reckoning they were well within the range of the Ceylon-based R.A.F. reconnaissance planes. It might even be the longed-for Catalina flying boat of Coastal

Command that Lind had dreamed would lift them out of the *Djohanis*.

Rowley voiced the view of them all as he listened to the plane's engine.

'Surely any plane we see now must be an ally,' he said.

'Shirts off,' said Jock and they all began to unbutton their shirts so that the R.A.F. pilot could see their white skins. Waller shook out the Union Jack and prepared to wave it in the wind.

It was Rowley who spotted the plane first. He looked at it doubtfully.

'I don't know this one,' he said, 'and personally I don't like the look of it.'

Waller, his habitual pessimism deserting him, turned to Rowley and said loftily. 'It's all right, it's one of those new American single-engine fighters.' But the words were hardly out of his mouth when the plane banked and they saw, unmistakably, the blood red circles of the Rising Sun on its wings.

Waller, who had been waving the Union Jack, dropped it hurriedly.

'Blimey,' thought Rowley. 'Now we really are for it.'

As the white men hastily retired to the cabin, raising the ventilator hatch in the atap roof to get a field of fire for their small arms, Jamal and Soon hurriedly took up their positions on the deck.

There was dissension in the cabin. Some were for taking on the plane, others counselled caution.

Spanton said, 'For God's sake don't shoot, you'll make him even more angry.'

For a moment it looked as though the subterfuge with the natives had worked. The plane pulled out of its dive and screamed over their heads and the two natives could see the pilot turn his head towards them. But as they watched the plane circled the *Djohanis* twice before banking in a sharp turn to come in, engines howling, in a low dive. Its guns were lined on the cabin. Rowley watched through the space between the hatch and the roof. He was sure that they had 'had it' and wondered only whether it would be bombs or guns that would end their escape.

For Jamal and Soon to have run across the open deck would have been madness so they dropped where they had stood and waited for the rattle of the guns. But there was no sound of guns. They waited, not daring to look up into the sky. They heard the plane climb, circle and dive once again. But again it roared over the boat and climbed back into its circle without firing a shot.

Unbelieving, the two natives heard the sound of the engine dying and, looking up, they saw the pilot wiggle his wings in a mocking salute as he disappeared into the distance.

The others were standing in a group by the door of the penthouse discussing the odd behaviour of the fighter. 'Perhaps he thought we weren't a sporting target,' someone suggested.

'More likely his guns jammed,' growled Doc who was not disposed to think kindly of his Imperial enemy and it was the Doc's solution that was accepted by most of the others. In their experience 'Bushido', the Japanese code of chivalry, was a romantic dream.

Rowley disagreed.

'It's a question of training,' he said. 'The Japanese have trained their army on German lines but their Navy is based on the British Navy. That's why their soldiers are such swine and their sailors behave so much better. That pilot was a sailor, obviously from an aircraft carrier. I think he believed we were ship-wrecked mariners and because he is a sailor himself he waved his wings to say "Good luck" and pushed off.'

It was a fanciful notion but the others agreed to give the sailor-pilot the benefit of the doubt.

The Doc was worried. He had noticed something that the others, apparently, had missed. It was something he chose to keep to himself for the moment. When the Japanese plane disappeared, presumably to return to its home base, it had been flying in the direction of Ceylon. The implications were shattering and he was relieved when as a spirit booster Jock Campbell ordered an extra ration of tea all round. Supposing Ceylon had fallen, what then? The thought of a friendly landfall was all that was keeping them going. What if they sailed into the harbour at Trincomalee to find themselves surrounded by Japanese shipping? Even if they spotted the danger from outside the harbour he doubted whether they had the resources or the rations to take them on to India itself. The Doc's hand shook as he reached for the tea and he was forced to beg for an extra cigarette from the *Djohanis*'s small store to supplement the one with which he had already been issued whilst the men waited anxiously for the return of the fighter-bomber.

Unaware of the dangers ahead the others concentrated their attention on a school of porpoises which had been following the *Djohanis* for several days. Now as they watched, the porpoises were joined by a small school of whales. After the empty days life of any kind was a welcome sight and they looked on with eager interest as the ponderous whales swam slowly in and out among the lively dolphins.

By this time they had become expert sailors. Long hours of practice had made them adept at handling the sails, even the cumbersome mainsail which had given them so much trouble in the early days of their voyage, and now, as Ivan held their course under a series of light squalls, they raised a full spread of canvas to catch every puff of wind.

That night in the Fo'c'sle club the Doc spoke of his fears for Ceylon. He was relieved when the others dismissed his theory that the Japanese was heading for a base on Ceylon itself. Although they did not know of the war being waged just over their horizon they argued that it was more likely that the Jap plane had flown from an aircraft carrier. But this theory, though it gave some relief to the Doc's troubled mind, opened up a harsher line of speculation. If the Japanese could operate so freely in the Indian Ocean where had our Navy gone? It was demoralizing even to consider the possibility of the Japanese navy operating in apparent immunity so near to British territory and that night a special double watch was kept for Japanese shipping and submarines.

The next day, 10 April, was livened by a series of squalls but that night when the moon rose the men felt the return of the North-Easter. The sails filled and the *Djohanis* was once again under way.

Gorham had been nervous since his last error of navigation and had lost confidence in the accuracy of his wrist watch. Hardly expecting a result he knelt down in front of the silent receiver and began half-heartedly to turn the knobs. Amazingly the radio replied at once with the faint strains of 'Roll out the Barrel', a Czechoslovakian drinking song which, in translation, had become one of the most popular of the wartime songs. Outside, the others caught the sound of the music riding over the crackle of interference and crowded into the penthouse to listen to the news. But the effort had been too much for the radio. Whatever freak pocket of energy it had found in the battery had been used up and even as they listened it spluttered, faded and died. Gorham's face was a study in baffled dismay. The music of 'Roll out the Barrel' had meant more to him than a link with the outside world. It was used, he knew, as a prelude to the Greenwich time signal. If that was what they had just heard his watch had gone wrong again. It added a further 50 miles to the 150 he had estimated they would still have to sail before they reached Ceylon. Infuriatingly there was no way of being sure. In the early days of the war the tune was played on almost every request programme. The others refused to be disquieted when Gorham confessed his fears and they tried to bolster up his diminishing self-confidence. Indeed they knew it would be difficult to fault a performance which had brought them, with little in the way of navigational aids, across a thousand miles of ocean.

The music might have been a soldier's request record. At their present rate of progress, their good-will argued, they would soon be in Ceylon. In a short time, they told him, they would be laughing at their fears over giant gins in a friendly wardroom.

The Doc did not share the general high spirits. For some days now he had been treating Ivan Lyon for lymphangitis. 'Patient!' thought Doc, the word had never been so inaccurately applied. Ivan was the most impatient of all the men he had treated since they left Sumatra. Now there were unmistakable signs that the disease was getting worse and the Doc wondered how long he would last before he would have to be relieved at the helm. That would be a job, he thought without enthusiasm. They'd have to knock Ivan out to get him to rest.

Brooke had contracted blood poisoning and was obviously in considerable pain but, like Ivan, was determined not to give in to his sickness and the Doc admired the way he insisted on carrying out his duties. To the Doc, despite the other man's war experience, he was still little more than a boy and he felt a quick stab of sympathy when he remembered Brooke's distress at being sea-sick before the others. These things mattered so much more when one was young.

His companions filled the Doc with admiration. More than anyone, he knew the stresses that such a voyage imposed on the human frame and so far the eighteen had come through the recurring crises of the trip incredibly well. The ten days of storms they had endured would have tried men with far greater experience of the sea. He watched them as they worked. Broome, more withdrawn now than he had been at the beginning of the trip, was, for all that, a quiet and efficient leader. He had shown great courage in climbing the mainmast in rough seas, a task which still filled the Doc with horror when he recalled it. Jock Campbell, also, was a born leader of men whose reserves of strength seemed inexhaustible. But the Doc's greatest admiration was reserved for

Ivan Lyon. He was superb and the doctor found it wonderfully reassuring to see him at the helm puffing contentedly at his pipe or chewing on one of the evil one-cent cigars which were part of the ship's stores. He was completely imperturbable and everyone on the ship had complete faith in him.

As the Doc went through the complement of the *Djohanis* one by one he applauded the shrewdness of Colonel Warren, who by now was almost certainly in a Japanese P.O.W. camp.

His musing was brought to an abrupt halt by a cry from the fo'c'sle.

'Man overboard,' the look-out called.

The Doc glanced over the side, just in time to see Douglas Fraser's feet threshing wildly in the air as he fell into the sea below. He saw the point of the anchor rip down Douglas's chin and blood spurt on to the hull. Fresh blood would attract the sharks, he thought in alarm, as he watched Douglas disappear under the surface. It seemed an age before his head, blood pouring from an angry wound in his face and staining the sea around him, came spluttering to the surface. Mercifully he came up near the boat and after several unsuccessful attempts managed to catch one of the ropes thrown to him and was hauled aboard. The Doc hurried to get his few medical supplies whilst Douglas lay in a pool of his own blood on the deck.

The anchor had ripped a gash in the right side of his chin. As he moved his head Rowley could see his teeth and the bone of the jaw which the gash exposed. He turned away involuntarily, nausea rising in his throat and when he turned back the Doctor was kneeling at Douglas's other side threading a sail needle with the thick thread they had been using to repair the canvas. Aghast he stared at the thread.

'What are you going to do with that?' he gasped.

'Sew up the gash, of course.'

'Well for God's sake give him some whisky,' pleaded Rowley. 'It's like a bloody harpoon.'

He took the whisky which someone handed to him and

raising it to Douglas's mouth tried to force it through his lips. Douglas had difficulty in swallowing and the whisky came pouring out of the gash in his cheek almost as fast as Rowley could pour it in. Rowley was not a squeamish man but the size of the sail needle had upset him. When he was sure that Douglas had swallowed some of the whisky he took a quick swig himself before he handed the bottle back to Jock.

The Doc looked up in amusement.

'Feel better now?'

Rowley nodded.

'Then perhaps we can begin.'

His stitches were deft and in next to no time the job was finished and the Doc was cutting the thread.

13

THE FRAGRANCE of the early morning tea rose in billows from the army mugs and the duty watch let it warm their faces. It had been a cold night and they shivered in the fresh dawn winds. But they had made good time through the night and, sleepy though they were, they were in high spirits. Sipping their tea, they looked on in amusement as Gorham emerged from the penthouse, yawned, stretched and made his way importantly to his navigation instruments. Gorham conducted his morning examination of the ship's position with a grave formality that brought grins to their faces. His inspection done, he crossed the deck to join them and cupped his hands round the mug that Soon handed him.

'Only 75 miles to go,' he said. 'I reckon we should be seeing some shipping any time now.'

Rowley was sceptical. He could not forget the earlier miscalculation and he had little respect for Gorham's erratic watch, whatever his opinion of him as a navigator.

'Are you sure?' he asked doubtfully.

'Sure?' bellowed Gorham. ' 'Course I'm sure. I brought you fifteen hundred miles, didn't I?'

Impishly Rowley goaded him.

'Checked your figures?'

Gorham tugged at his beard.

'Seventy-five miles, Rowley,' he said. 'Couple of days from now you'll be buying me large gins shore-side.'

Even for Gorham it was a bold statement and the rest of the watch looked at him doubtfully. But a moment later he was triumphantly vindicated by a warning shout from Ivan at the wheel.

'Tanker on the port bow,' he roared.

Tea and banter forgotten the men ran to the side to follow Lyon's pointing finger. Four or five miles away on the starboard bow they could see the long, grey hull of the distant tanker, steaming and pitching in the slow swell, dull now under a gathering squall. It was the first powered ship they had seen since they parted from the Dutchman's tug off the Sumatran coast and it seemed vast. The high bows, separated as they were by the low line of her midship tanks from the superstructure aft, made her appear like two ships.

'Isn't she beautiful,' breathed Douglas.

'And isn't she a long way off,' breathed Waller.

Soon they saw the plumed smokestack of a second ship and then a third.

'It's a bloody armada,' said Lind. 'Let's make a signal.'

Jock Campbell was uneasy.

'Let's hold off for a bit,' he cautioned. 'They may be Japs. They aren't showing any colours, and they're sailing East.'

It was a chilling thought and it brought silence to the excited group. Gorham alone was scornful.

'It's impossible,' he said. 'They wouldn't sail unarmed merchantmen without an escort in British waters.'

'How do we know they are British waters?' asked Jock quietly, and Doc, remembering the plane that had flown in the direction of Ceylon, shuddered. Supposing Ceylon had fallen like Malaya and the Dutch East Indies. If impregnable Singapore could fall with such ease why not Ceylon?

Doc knew how important it was that the voyage end soon. He was worried by the mounting tensions in the crew. Thankfully the health of the sicklier ones had improved and the men were fitter than they had been at any time during the voyage but the nervous strain was beginning to tell on constitutions already taxed to their limit. If Ceylon was indeed in enemy hands their only hope was to sail on until they reached the coast of Africa but he doubted whether the crew had strength left to take the *Djohanis* round an enemy-held coastline and across thousands of miles of ocean. Even if the men could make it they had not enough provisions for such a journey. Their only hope lay in the tankers.

'I think we should make the signal,' he said.

The younger men who had been arguing in favour of attracting the tanker's attention looked at him in surprise; they had not hoped for support from one of the older members of the company. Broome glanced at him irresolutely but he read something of the other's thoughts and he made up his mind quickly.

'Make a signal,' he said.

It was easier to say than to accomplish. They had no usable flares and they dare not loose off a burst from a machine gun in case the tankers mistook their intention and blew them out of the water. Broome decided to hoist a makeshift distress signal of a basket covered with the blue ensign and a grey blanket. For better or for worse the decision had been made and they waited anxiously to see what would happen. They waited in vain. No one on the tankers saw the signal and, helplessly, the men watched the ships steam over the horizon.

Brooke could not hide his scorn.

'Bloody Merchant Navy. No look-outs,' he gibed at Gorham. Doc noticed with concern that he was only half-joking. Nerves were on edge again and the goodwill of the morning had totally vanished.

Although they did not know it they had just been through the most dangerous moments of the entire voyage. The tankers were indeed Japanese. They had been refuelling the task force in the Bay of Bengal and were returning to their home bases. Forty-eight hours after they were spotted by the

Djohanis the tankers picked up another boat-load of survivors from Sumatra. Among them was Colonel Dillon, the officer who had been in charge of the rubber factory in Sumatra. After a thousand-mile voyage to freedom they spent the rest of the war in a series of Jap P.O.W. camps.

Unaware of their narrow escape, Gorham thought of Rowley's jibes. Supposing his watch was wrong and his calculations were out once again. He shaded his eyes, searching for the first sign of the coast of Ceylon which, according to his reckoning, should have come into sight by now.

He was a good navigator. He knew that. To bring a craft the size of the *Djohanis* so far with such woefully inadequate navigation aids was an incredible feat of seamanship—an old atlas, a creaking mast and a torn sail, a flat and useless radio and on top of it all that damned watch. Every minute it lost put them fifteen miles off-course. He stared moodily at a bank of cloud which rested heavily on the horizon. He looked again, and what he saw made him turn and beckon to Jock Campbell. Jock had seen Gorham stiffen and had followed his eyes to the horizon. He crossed to his side.

'What is it?' he asked.

'That cloud on the horizon. I'm pretty certain it isn't a cloud at all. It's Adam's Peak.'

'It's Ceylon.'

Campbell's heart leapt and his stomach felt hollow. But he forced himself to remain outwardly calm and shading his eyes like his companion he stared at the horizon. He thought Gorham was mistaken. The grey mass looked to him like a cloud formation. At any moment it will break up, he told himself. He was glad he had not called to the others who were eating lunch under the shade of the penthouse.

'I'm afraid it is cloud,' he told Gorham. 'Although it does look . . .' He paused. By now, surely, the cloud should have broken or at least changed outline. But it had not. The shape on the horizon was rigid, its edge broken in mist. It was not cloud. It was land.

'It *is* land,' he said unbelievingly. 'Land, land.' His voice rose and Gorham hugged him in delight, his huge black-bearded face split in an enormous grin. Soon the two men were shouting to the others.

The men had looked up from their meal in astonishment. It was utterly out of character for Jock to shout. Then they heard the word for which they had waited so long and they jumped to their feet, food forgotten. They raced for the side and followed Gorham's excited directions until they saw the grey smudge far away on the horizon. Not that they could see a great deal, thought Rowley. It was just a blur on an otherwise depressingly dull horizon. As land went, it did not go very far. He hoped it would not disappear altogether.

Holly was quite unmoved by the sighting. When Rowley turned he saw that the venerable white-bearded chairman of the Fo'c'sle club had not joined in the general rush for the side of the boat when the cry had gone up. He was sitting now, placidly mopping up the last of his luncheon bully from the bottom of his tin plate with the scraps of an army biscuit. As he munched he watched with well-bred indulgence the antics of the younger members of the party. Rowley walked over to sit at his side.

'You don't seem to be very excited,' he said.

'I never like to rush about in the middle of a meal. It's so bad for the digestion,' replied Holly.

The others noticed him sitting in the shade of the penthouse and called him to join them. Holly smiled and raised a hand but he refused to move until the last scrap of luncheon had been finished and the tea drunk.

'That was very good,' he said. 'Now let's see what all the fuss is about.'

Rowley was amazed by Holly's self-possession as he slowly got to his feet and strolled over to the ship's side where his companions vied to be the first to point out the land to him. His response, though friendly, was cool.

'Oh,' he said, 'land. Very nice.' And with that he turned and rejoined Rowley in the shade of the cabin.

'They're making a lot of fuss,' he said with just a hint of disapproval.

One other man did not share in the general high spirits. Ivan Lyon silently watched the others slapping each other in their excitement. Doc realised that as helmsman Ivan must have seen the land before any of them but he had kept the secret until it was confirmed by Gorham, the look-out. Not for the first time Doc marvelled at the self-control of the small, bird-like man. After a month of living cheek by jowl he felt that at the end of the voyage he knew as little of Ivan as he had known when they met for the first time on the verandah of Colonel Warren's house in Padang. He wondered what thoughts had been running through the mind of the little Highlander as he stood hour after hour, day after day, in his own small world, curiously apart from the rest of the party.

A strange thought struck the Doc. It remained in his mind and he mentioned it when he came to write the diary of the voyage of the *Djohanis*.

> Typical of Ivan's calmness was the fact that he sighted Ceylon about three hours before anyone else.
>
> He refrained from saying anything until he was absolutely certain, though some of the party had a shrewd suspicion that he kept silent in order to prolong the sailing trip which he was so obviously enjoying.

Ivan, alone of the eighteen, was sorry the trip was over.

That afternoon the wind fell and the *Djohanis* drifted in flat calm, the plaything of currents that toyed with her and then abandoned her. The younger men were in agonies of impatience. Hanging from the rigging, perched on the bow, leaning from every conceivable vantage point they scoured the horizon for signs of shipping or strained to see Adam's Peak. Its distant outline taunted them and it was in vain that the older men warned them that there might still be days of drifting before their ordeal was over. The taste of land, teasing them on the sea's edge, had filled them with longing and the light North-Easter which sprang up at 1700 hours on the 12th increased their impatience. As they watched them the older men waited for the depression they knew must follow the euphoria of the first sighting. But with land waiting for them nothing the others could say would serve to calm the high spirits of the younger men.

Jock was worried.

'We've got to think of something to take their minds off the land,' he said to the Doc. Then an idea struck him and his face lit up.

'We'll have a party,' he told the astonished Doctor. 'A successful crossing of the Indian Ocean in this battered old tub should be worth some sort of celebration, surely?'

He searched about in his mind for something with which to celebrate their achievement; something so special that it would stand out in their memories. At last he had it.

'We'll open the tin of tomato soup,' he said.

The Doc could hardly believe his ears. The tin of tomato soup, the only one in the stores, occupied, he knew, a special place in Jock's heart and he had been deaf to pleas from the others to open it ever since they set sail from Sumatra.

'Are you sure?'

'Aye, I think so.'

When Jock announced his decision the rest of the crew shared the doctor's disbelief.

The menu was a delight and the men went over it lovingly as they skipped through their morning's work. Tomato soup. They could feel its special sharpness on their tongues and for hours they discussed whether they should mix it with condensed milk and water to stretch it further or demolish it in one exquisite mouthful. Prudence prevailed and they decided to dilute it. The meal was to be the largest they had eaten since the voyage began; for once Jock had made up his mind his prodigality was boundless. The men were astonished to learn that there were to be no less than four tins of bully beef and, unheard of luxury, a tin of tomatoes, a tin of carrots AND a tin of potatoes. They were even to have dessert. Two slices of tinned pear and a teaspoonful of condensed milk for each man and to end the meal two buttered biscuits and two-thirds of a pint of coffee.

That afternoon they spent preparing for the feast. Beards were trimmed with the only pair of scissors on board, moustaches plucked into order and torn uniforms neatly darned. Even Rowley took an uncomplaining turn with the needle and when at last evening fell they were already seated cross-legged in happy expectancy.

When the soup arrived they fell on it with enthusiasm. It had been so long since any of them had tasted soup it was as though they were experiencing it for the first time. Too soon it was gone and they handed up their plates for the next course. The Doc was staggered at the quantity. Used as he had become to short rations the portion of bully beef seemed enormous and the tomatoes, potatoes and carrots vivid in their colouring and plenty. He thought wryly that what in pre-war days he would have considered a light luncheon now seemed a banquet and the thought of eating such a great pile of food himself utter greed. His musings must have been shared by the others for he noticed the enthusiasm with which they had greeted the soup had waned and they munched now almost as a duty. Although they brightened with the dessert it was obvious they were struggling when the biscuits were served and they grabbed at the coffee with relief.

Ten small tins of food had proved too much for the eighteen. Their stomachs felt distended and when the meal was over they stretched out where they sat, too full of food to move, and some with the rumbles of indigestion. Presently they began to feel livelier and they lay swapping stories of their lives before the war. That night the Fo'c'sle Club held a musical evening and for two hours their voices and the lonely harmony of Holly's banjo rang out over the ocean around them.

When dawn came and they looked towards the horizon their high spirits evaporated in an instant. The coastline had vanished. All round them, once again, was the vast empty Indian Ocean. Worse, a strong South-Westerly had blown up in the night and was now driving them away from Ceylon. Ivan fought to take every advantage of wind and current but the dull *Djohanis* responded slowly and their hopes faded.

Jock Campbell watched the others anxiously. They wore their despondency like blankets round their shoulders. The well-being of the night before was gone and once again tempers flared at the smallest provocation. Since the fall of Singapore they had survived test after test. The fact that they were on the *Djohanis* at all was proof of how successfully they had survived the ordeals they had faced. But this final blow brought them to their knees. More than anything else now they were angry that they had not seen either the Royal Navy nor the Royal Air Force when they had expected to see regular patrols in and above the shipping lanes. Tojo was crushed at their new misfortune and he lay in the penthouse, uncaring, his face turned to the cabin wall. Jock knew that it would not be long before the others were sharing his despair.

The day, as it wore on, brought more worries. Although Brooke and Lyon were recovering from their lymphangitis, Davis' ulcers, the Doctor noticed, were turning septic.

At 1100 on 14 April they saw a wisp of smoke on the rim of the sea and in a short while they were able to make out the outline of another tanker. Once again they hoisted their makeshift distress signal and Brooke tried to heliograph the ship with a broken mirror. It was no use. As they watched the smoke on the horizon grew fainter until at last it vanished altogether.

It was obvious to Broome and Campbell that a decision about their future would have to be made quickly and a meeting of all hands was called. When they assembled Gorham told them in a few words of their position.

'We're making for the Great Basses Light,' he told them. 'But so far it has not come into view. The coast nearest to our present position is rocky and uninhabited. Landing there will be dangerous and the *Djohanis* could easily be smashed by the breakers against the rocky coral. 'I don't see what else we can do, though,' he added. 'Our chances of being picked up by a ship seem to be small.'

Rowley led those members of the party who were against landing at any cost. He put his point of view with uncharacteristic brevity. 'If the water here is thirty feet deep then I can swim thirty feet—straight down,' he said. 'And I haven't spent a month at sea and crossed 1,500 miles of ocean to drown off the coast of Ceylon.'

The soldiers aboard agreed with Rowley but the sailors were unanimously in favour of trying to make the landing. In a moment the first major disagreement of the trip had broken out as tempers rose and individual dislikes, carefully guarded until now, became apparent. It was a dangerous moment and it took the combined efforts of Jock and the Doctor to bring peace between the two factions.

The Doc tried to put both points of view quietly and with reasoned arguments. 'There are risks in trying to get ashore, true,' he said. 'But are they greater than allowing ourselves to be picked up by ships not flying national flags? It would be the worst kind of luck to be found by a Japanese vessel when we've come so far and are so near our destination.'

Late in the afternoon they saw the coast again. It was nearer now and they could make out the contours of the cliffs and distant palm trees; and still the argument continued, with Rowley acting as spokesman for the soldiers and Gorham leading the sailors. At length, though still unconvinced, Rowley allowed himself to be persuaded to have a look at the shore and Ivan Lyon changed to a course which would bring them near enough to inspect the coastline. When they were half a mile offshore and Rowley was able to see the dangers ahead his heart sank. It was far worse than even he had imagined. Even the sailors, who a little while before had been loud in their arguments in favour of landing, stood hushed in awe at the formidable sight before them. Great mountains of surf crashed on rocks like bayonets and buffeted the thirty-foot-high cliffs. Any one of the rollers would have smashed the *Djohanis* into fragments against the rocks.

'This is crazy,' Rowley stormed. 'You're throwing all our lives away. We'll never be able to land through that. Those waves start in the Antarctic.'

He gestured at the boiling sea as it battered the rocky beach below the cliffs and even the sailors were bound to agree. Landing at the point for which they were making was plainly out of the question and they agreed another try should be made along the coast for a safer anchorage.

They were barely under way when Holly's cry of 'Mine' brought everyone to join him and a little ahead of them they saw a sinister dark dish bobbing in the swell. There was no way they could avoid it.

The wind was blowing them directly into its path and it seemed that, after all, they would have been better to have risked the surf. Then, just as a collision seemed inevitable, the 'Mine' shook itself and with an audible sigh disappeared under the surface of the water!

'It was only a bloody fish,' said Rowley, relieved.

Rowley was feeling better now. Privately he thought their chances of being able to sail into a harbour were remote and he reckoned the odds were on their being picked up by a boat of some kind long before they tried a landing party. His relief when at last a tanker appeared on the horizon was manifest.

'A ship,' he called. 'A lovely great ship.'

The others followed his pointing finger. The ship was not flying any distinguishing flags and once again there was no way in which they could tell if she was friend or foe.

'She's large and she's certainly armed,' the Doc said. 'But

surely she wouldn't be on her own without an escort in these waters unless she was an ally? This is very much Britain's back yard.'

'It was, you mean,' Holly said. 'For all we know it could be Japan's front garden now.'

From the poop Ivan Lyon broke in.

'There is little time left before the decision is taken out of our hands,' he said quietly. 'What's it to be? Ship or shore?'

As one they looked at the reassuring hulk of the ship, its great bow slicing through the seas, independent of favourable winds or capricious currents. Then they looked at the perilous coast with its needles of rock and furious breakers. Anything was preferable to that.

'Ship,' they said with one voice.

'Ship it is,' said Ivan and prepared to take the *Djohanis* across the bows of the tanker.

Minutes later, from the activity on the bridge, they knew that they had been spotted. It was with profound relief that, shortly afterwards, they made out the name *Anglo-Canadian* which still showed under the grey paint which covered her bows.

'She's British,' Gorham shouted in delight. 'British Merchant Navy,' he added, glaring at the R.N. men. 'That means there's a fair chance we'll get aboard without being run down.'

'Get the distress signals up,' shouted Broome. 'She doesn't look too sure of us.'

The sailors amongst them had insisted that a round ball in the mast was the correct distress signal and had lashed one together with lengths of cane. Rowley grabbed an Aldis lamp and started to signal to the ship while everyone else was rummaging amongst his belongings for clothing that could be used as signals. The shirts, flags and spare bunting looked more like a laundry line than an appeal for help. In the event it nearly cost them their lives.

14

ON THE bridge of the *Anglo-Canadian*, Captain Williams from Aberystwyth looked through his glasses doubtfully at the curious wooden craft which was crossing his bows. Two days earlier they had been bombed in Vizagapatam by a Japanese bomber force. Seven British ships had been sunk. The one direct hit on the stern of the *Canadian* had failed to explode but every one on the merchantman was on edge and ready for trouble.

The Captain turned to his Number One.

'What d'you make of her?'

The Number One focused his binoculars. 'Looks harmless enough, but it could be a trick. Hang on, sir. They're making a signal.'

He watched in bewilderment as one by one the shirts and the flags made their uncertain way up the rigging of the *Djohanis*. With difficulty the Number One picked out the message the fishing boat was spelling. It was unbelievable. He lowered his glasses in amazement and rubbed them to clear the lens. Then, his eyes screwed in astonishment at what he had seen, he raised the binoculars again and focused on the rigging. He had not been mistaken. The message was still there. He shook his head.

'What is it?' asked Skipper Williams, impatiently.

'That little boat, sir,' said the Number One weakly, 'is signalling that she is preparing to attack.'

Unlikely adversary though the *Djohanis* appeared the skipper had heard of suicide missions and this could be one of them. He could not afford to take risks with his cargo and his barked order brought sailors running from all over the ship.

'Action stations!'

The order had been given many times on the *Anglo-Canadian* and it was obeyed with the smooth efficiency that comes with constant practice. The merchantman slackened speed and made a half circle which brought her sweeping round in a wide arc. The men on the *Djohanis* stared at her open-mouthed.

On the *Canadian*'s after-deck there was a gun and it was trained menacingly on the penthouse of their craft. Rowley looked doubtfully at the impressive barrel which was pointing down at them. He was uneasily aware of the angry glares he was getting from those of his companions who had wanted to try to land on the coast.

Suddenly through a loud hailer he heard an unmistakably Welsh accent.

'If you don't take your washing down,' the voice came across the water, 'you're liable to be blown out of the water.'

The naval contingent and Gorham were for once united in their sheepishness as they took down the offending signal and as a precaution against further misunderstanding Jamal and Soon were sent below.

'That's better,' said the Captain. 'Now bring her alongside and let's get a better look at you.'

'That's a bit thick,' said Brooke. 'After we've come all this way one would have thought they would have come alongside us.'

For Ivan the long sail was over. He brought the *Djohanis* alongside the rope ladders which had been thrown over the merchantman's side. It was a tricky manoeuvre and it took nearly an hour to complete under sail, but at last it was over and with it the long voyage to freedom. In 36 days, 13 hours and 31 minutes the *Djohanis* had sailed at an average speed of 1·89 knots, a distance of 1,659 miles and the Doctor was delighted to observe that when she was tied alongside the *Anglo-Canadian* all her crew were fit enough to climb unaided up a thirty-foot rope ladder to the welcoming hands that waited to pull them aboard.

Waller was dancing in delight at the realization that all his gloomy forebodings had been vanquished. There had been nothing negative about Waller's pessimism, it was a full-blooded animal which he fed with relish. But as he waited his turn on the rope ladder he quickly banished it from his mind. He was still laughing happily when he fell into the sea. He was soon helped back on to the *Djohanis*'s deck, spluttering and soaked but he had taken the lesson to heart and as he climbed the rope ladder he turned to those still waiting below.

'You see,' he said with the air of a man who has learned his lesson, 'It's never wise to look on the bright side.'

Aboard the *Anglo-Canadian* a tumultuous welcome awaited them. The whole ship's company had turned out to cheer. Lind was given the loudest ovation. He had been off-watch and asleep when the tanker had been sighted. Instinctively when he awoke and saw the gun of the merchantman trained on the *Djohanis* he had reached for his steel helmet. But in the excitement of the minutes that had followed he had forgotten the rest of his clothes.

Captain Williams came down from the bridge to meet the men from the *Djohanis* which now bobbed unacknowledged thirty foot below them. They were a piratical lot, he thought, with their tattered clothes and festooned with rifles, machine guns and mills bombs.

He introduced himself to them all, 'Captain Williams from Aberystwyth.'

As they shook hands Rowley told him, 'I'm a Welshman too.'

'Where from?'

'I'm afraid you wouldn't know it. It's a little place called Rhuddlan.'

'Know it?' said the skipper. 'I never hear of anything else. My Chief Engineer comes from the same village.'

He turned to a seaman who was standing nearby.

'Go and tell Mr Le Frenais I've got a neighbour of his called to see him. Dropped in, you might say.'

Later over the steaming mugs of boiling tea of which they had dreamed for so long the eighteen were made to go over every detail of their adventure for the ship's officers. Everyone enjoyed himself according to his lights. Rowley thought they were the most appreciative audience he had ever had whilst Douglas was in raptures over the sandwiches. When at length their story was over and the last question asked and answered the Skipper brought them round to the *Djohanis*.

'What are we going to do with her?' he asked.

'How do you mean?' the Doc asked.

'Well,' said the skipper, 'we can hardly bring her aboard and take her to Ceylon, and we can't let her float about in the shipping lanes. She could be a danger to other shipping.'

He paused. He knew that what he was going to say next would not please the eighteen men around him. Very gently he went on:

'I'm afraid the only thing we can do is to sink her.'

The men were horrified. They knew every mood of the prahu and but for her they would be in a P.O.W. camp in Sumatra. It was hard that she should be sunk after she had brought them through so much to safety.

'Couldn't we take her in tow?' one asked.

The skipper shrugged. 'What would you do with her when you landed in Ceylon? You can't be dragging a great fishing boat round with you, man.'

Unpalatable though it was they could see the force of the Captain's argument.

'Look,' he said. 'I'm a sailor and I know what it is to love your ship, but there are times when you can't be sentimental. We cannot just let her drift. Some ship might run into her in the dark. Her skipper wouldn't know she's empty and he might waste hours looking for her crew. Long enough anyway for the Japs to get him. I'm sorry, gentlemen; very sorry. But your prahu will have to go.'

* * *

On deck the eighteen men watched as a sailor cut the *Djohanis* adrift. Teased by a favourable wind her sails shook and she was soon curvetting away, free to follow the caprice of her own whim.

For the gun crews on the *Anglo-Canadian* she presented an easy target and the first shot from the 12 pounder in the ship's stern tore through her rigging. The second, a direct hit, brought a smile to the Doc's lips.

'That'll be a nasty surprise for the cockroaches,' he said.

Curiously the shelling was having little or no effect on the *Djohanis*. The men who had crossed the Indian Ocean in her watched with amazement as one by one she took the shells, then, her mast dipping, she shook like a boxer absorbing a pummelling.

'She's not going to sink,' said Rowley. 'She's going to beat them.'

'How can she?' said Waller. 'She's only timber; she's bound to break up.'

But the *Djohanis* did not break up. The last glimpse the men she had brought so far had of the little boat was of her silhouette as she sailed into a blood-red sunset.

That night, in the luxury of a comfortable bunk, the Doc wrote her epitaph in his diary. When he had finished he laid his pen aside and read what he had written:

The S/V *Djohanis* was then shelled by the 12 pounder

listened to the news bulletins on the radio. The news was disheartening but at least they were alive to listen to it.

At last, after five days, as dawn broke on Sunday, 19 April, the *Anglo-Canadian* steamed into the Bombay Roads. The long adventure was nearly over and all eighteen were on deck to see the approach of land. Lying before them and stretching almost as far as the eye could see, was the British fleet. They saw the *Indefatigable*, the *Indomitable* and the *Warspite*. Flotilla after flotilla, almost every kind of warship rode at anchor in the roads. Everyone was impressed except Gorham. His glistening black beard bristled as he surveyed the grey menace which lay in its might all about him.

'Idle bastards,' he said contemptuously. 'I'll bet they're all at an Admiral's cocktail party. It's only the Merchant Navy that goes to sea in wartime.'

From its anchorage in the outer roads the *Anglo-Canadian* signalled the news of the arrival of the men from the *Djohanis* to an aircraft-carrier anchored nearby. After a long time the men saw a small craft being launched from the aircraft-carrier and watched its white wake as it headed for the *Anglo-Canadian*. The launch had authority to take off the R.N. and R.N.V.R. personnel but Gorham refused to go.

'Thank you,' he said with icy dignity when he was offered a place. 'I think I'll stick with the army. I feel safer.'

15

ROWLEY WATCHED as the launch containing the naval party approached the aircraft carrier. Before the R.N. men left they had arranged to meet for a celebration dinner with the Captain and Officers of the *Anglo-Canadian* in the Taj Mahal, the largest hotel in Bombay. But first for the soldiers there was the problem of getting ashore themselves. With Rowley to think was to act and accordingly he made his way to the bridge.

'Well, skipper,' he said as he came into the wheelhouse, 'What about one of your ship's boats for us?'

Williams was aghast. 'Ship's boat?' he said. 'We can't lower those. It's against Board of Trade regulations.'

Rowley looked at him in dismay. So far as he could see no one on the shore was making any effort to take them off and it was too far to swim. He went back and held a conference with the others and then led them in a body to the Captain.

'What are we going to do?' the doctor asked.

'Oh, don't worry,' the skipper reassured him. 'There's bound to be a bumboat alongside anytime now. You can go ashore in that.'

It was a bit hard, Rowley thought. They had escaped from the Japanese, sailed for over a month across the Indian Ocean and now they were being asked to land in a bumboat. He had not expected brass bands but he could not help feeling that something more enthusiastic in the way of a welcome was in order. He turned to Jock Campbell for support.

'Don't worry, Rowley,' said Jock. 'We'll soon be home now. Look, there's a boat coming alongside now.'

Below them in a long narrow rowing boat an old man and a boy were looking up at the rail of the *Anglo-Canadian*.

'Now's your chance to practise your Urdu,' said Jock. 'Tell them we want to go ashore.'

Rowley leaned over the ship's side and called down to the old man in his best British Army Urdu.

'Will you take us ashore?' he asked.

'Oh most certainly, sahib,' the man replied. 'You have Indian money?' he added.

'That's torn it,' said Spanton. 'All we've got is a few guilders.'

It was ridiculous, thought Rowley. Forty-two days at sea and the only welcome they were getting was an argument over money with an Indian boatman.

'Plenty of money,' he called. 'Now stand by we're going to lower a ladder.'

But the old boatman had been working the Bombay waterfront too long to be caught by such a ruse. He stood in the boat and raised a hand to halt the sailors as they prepared to throw down the rope ladder.

'First you show me Indian money,' he said with finality.

Rowley refused to be beaten. 'We've got Dutch money,' he told the Indian. 'Very good money. Better than Indian money.'

The boatman was unimpressed. 'Dutch money no good in Bombay Harbour,' he replied flatly.

Exasperation mounted in Rowley's voice.

'All right, we'll get some when we land. We will change our Dutch money into Indian money.'

'For ten rupees Indian money?' the boatman asked doubtfully.

Rowley estimated the going rate was two rupees for the journey but it was a seller's market.

'All right,' he said, 'ten rupees.'

It was getting towards lunch-time and he longed for the taste of a pre-luncheon gin and tonic.

Satisfied, the boatman caught hold of the rope ladder and steadied it whilst the soldiers, after saying goodbye to the crew, climbed down into the bumboat.

The boatman looked with little favour when the barefooted Rowley and his heavily armed companions settled into the boat. It was obvious that he had made a bad bargain and plainly he could foresee difficulties about the ten rupees when they landed. He looked balefully at the guns but with a sigh, he pushed off from the side of the ship.

'Where do you wish to go?' he asked.

'Where do the British soldiers usually land,' Rowley returned.

'At Ballard Pier,' said the boatman.

'Then that will do splendidly,' said Rowley and lay back in the boat with an air which told the boatman the conversation was at an end.

If the boatman had been suspicious, the Indian customs official who peered down at them from the pier was positively hostile. The men below him were not wearing uniform yet they were bristling with guns and looked dangerous.

He watched apprehensively as they clambered up to the pier, looking about them and chatting amiably, ignoring his presence.

Indian customs officials are not accustomed to being ignored.

'What do you want?' he said in a loud, official voice. 'You cannot land here without authorisation. Have you authorisation?'

Jock Campbell fixed him with an iron glare.

'We have come from Sumatra,' he said 'and we had more important things to do than hunt for landing papers.'

So far as the Indian official was concerned the incident was closed by Jock's admission.

'If you have not an authorisation you cannot land,' he told them. 'You must go back.'

It was a hell of a welcome, thought Rowley crossly. The whole business was becoming a crazy nightmare.

'Look,' he said with forced patience. 'We've just escaped from Singapore and frankly I don't think going back would be an awfully good idea. Surely there is some sort of form you can give us to fill in.'

Forms were something the customs official understood. He rummaged amongst a pile of documents in his brief case and triumphantly produced one which covered the circumstances. As the men watched in amazement he slowly unscrewed the cap of an elderly fountain pen, shook it and licked the nib, with becoming gravity.

'What are your names?' he asked 'and the numbers of your fire-arms.'

There was nothing else for it. One by one the soldiers answered the endless questions the customs official asked them. By now they had abandoned any dreams they may have had of a heroes' welcome and they just wanted to slink quietly away for a restoring drink. But the last question took them by surprise.

'What is your reason for landing?'

It was too much. Rowley threw up his hands in despair and turned to Jock for support.

Jock grinned. 'What about "lack of co-operation with Japanese New Order in Asia," ' he said. It was the phrase the Japanese always used to enable them to punish the people who opposed them.

It had a fine ringing sound and the customs official happily wrote down the phrase as Jock dictated it to him, in the appropriate space on the form. Next he took a note of the numbers on their weapons. Then, the formalities completed and honour satisfied, he beamed and bowed slightly.

'Welcome to British India,' he said with dignity.

This touching ceremony was more than a little marred by an aggrieved voice from the back of the little group.

'You owe me ten rupees,' it said pettishly.

They had forgotten the boatman but they now saw he was determined to stay with them until he had received payment of the money he considered to be his due.

'Lord knows,' said Rowley visibly put out. 'I didn't expect a gong and tea with the Viceroy but I do think they could have done a little better than this.'

'Come on,' said Jock. 'We'd better make our number with District Headquarters and let them sort things out. Ask your nice friend in the customs if he will lend us two annas for the phone call.'

The customs official was reluctant. The presence of an unsatisfied creditor in the person of the visibly agitated boatman had done little to establish their credit in his eyes. But at last he was prevailed upon to loan them the money and the party made their way to a telephone box.

It was agony. In the mid-day sun the pavements were baking hot and they sizzled under Rowley's bare feet as he walked.

'Blimey,' he exploded, 'it's like walking on hot coals.'

And as the others watched helpless with laughter the little gunner, festooned with his various arms, hopped in agony and made quick darts from one pool of shade across the baking pavements to the next, pursued by a determined boatman calling in a shrill voice:

'You pay me my ten rupees. Where is my ten rupees, sahib?'

* * *

The Duty Officer of District Command Headquarters, Bombay, on that April Sunday morning was a man used to the wiles of his fellow officers and the ruses they employed to borrow transport to get back to their units after leave. By any standards the story he had just been told was the most improbable he had ever heard.

'You've come from where?' he said languidly down the telephone. 'Come off it, old man...'

At the other end of the phone Jock was on the verge of apoplexy.

'You damn fool, I tell you we've just come from Singapore. If you aren't prepared to send transport of some kind I'll bloody well ring off and speak to the District Commander himself.'

'For God's sake don't ring off,' whispered Douglas urgently. 'We haven't any more money to ring anyone else.'

Fortunately the duty officer was beginning to believe the story.

'Well I can send transport for the officers,' he conceded at last, 'but not for the other ranks. If there are other ranks with you they cannot use it.'

Jock looked out of the telephone box at Jamal and Soon who had stood so bravely on the exposed deck during the attacks by the Japanese planes.

'We're all officers here,' he said shortly.

At last a three tonner arrived. They borrowed ten rupees from the driver to pay the boatman and the party climbed in for the six mile ride to Colaba Reinforcement Camp. At the gate Jock, the only one who still had his officer's cap, got out of the truck first.

A sentry took one look at the piratical crew which followed him, Gorham with his bristling black beard, Rowley in a green felt hat, Douglas in a medley of civilian clothes and Spanton as always beautifully turned out, and called out the Guard Sergeant.

From the sergeant the group were passed on quickly to the adjutant who in his turn took them to the Commanding Officer.

When they trooped into his tent the C.O. was so smart from his shining shoes to his crisply starched uniform that he took the escapees breath away. Spanton regarded him with approval.

He listened as his adjutant outlined their recent history and then he broke in.

'Mac, I think we want fifteen bottles of beer here at once, followed by another fifteen in ten minutes' time. Will you tell the Mess there will be ten guests for luncheon in about three-quarters of an hour and will you then say that I shall want the Camp Quartermaster and the Camp Paymaster here at 2 o'clock and 2.30 respectively.'

Rowley's sigh of relief was audible. They were home. They were back in the system once more.

* * *

The foam of the cherry blossom had died in Kashmir while the battle of Singapore had raged and now the fruit hung in clusters from the branches, out of reach of the children below. But they waited patiently for they knew the soldier would be coming soon and they would presently be eating their fill of the cherries.

The Shalimar Gardens had been perfect that May and Rowley heartily agreed with a motto he found engraved on a stone. It read:

'If there is a heaven on earth it is this, it is this, it is this...'

The motto ran through his head as he cantered his horse towards the cherry orchard and the waiting children. His leave pass had arrived only ten days earlier and he had made at once for Kashmir, which was to become his favourite place in all India.

He smiled to himself as he thought of the frantic days which had followed the landing in Ceylon. Their pockets full of pay they had gone on a great spending spree and he had got through £200 in less than a week on food, drink, uniform and hand-made shoes. The men from the *Djohanis* had bought a silver cigarette box engraved with a picture of their prahu and they presented it to the officers of the *Anglo-Canadian* at a celebration dinner.

Rowley winced when he remembered the dinner. The Taj Mahal Hotel was having difficulty in maintaining its standards in war-time and the meal they were given was atrocious. The French and German wines had all been drunk and they could only get Australian wine and even worse Australian whisky. But it had been a jolly meal and for all its shortcomings a great improvement on the cups of rice on which they had survived for so long.

One by one in the week that followed the men who had been together for so long were swallowed up in the army machine. For Ivan Lyon tragedy was only days away. He learned that his wife and child were in Australia and he managed to get himself a posting there at much the same time as his wife had arranged her own passage to India. Their ships passed and some days later the one in which his wife and child were sailing was torpedoed. Both were missing.

It made him more determined than ever to carry out the plan he had formed on the *Djohanis*. Incredibly under his messianic guidance the plan became a reality and on 9 August, 1943, he sailed out of the mouth of the Barron River in North Queensland with a team of the finest frogmen the army could collect.

By one of the strangest coincidences of the war the fishing boat in which they sailed was the same battered *Ko Fuku Maru* which Rowley and Douglas had coveted during the rescue operations in Sumatra and in which Captain Bill Reynolds had sailed to safety.

Renamed the *Krait* and refitted and armoured she was taken by Lyon first to Exmouth Gulf on the coast of Western Australia, a voyage in itself of 2,400 miles. And by a further coincidence the *Krait* sailed eighteen months to the night that the *Djohanis* had started her voyage from Padang.

She carried fourteen men, four of them soldiers, the rest sailors. Her No. 4 hold and eight 44 gallon drums strapped to her deck held enough fuel for a cruising range of 13,000 miles.

The route for Operation Jaywick, as the raid was called, was from the Exmouth Gulf, across the Indian Ocean and through the enemy-held Lombok Straits to the Java coast. From there the *Krait* went along the coast of Borneo, through the Rhio Archipelago to the coastal waters of Singapore. And there whilst the Japanese slept, frogmen from the *Krait* sank or damaged nearly 39,111 tons of enemy shipping in the harbour.

Ivan brought the party back to safety in Australia but he could not rest. On 11 September that year he mounted a second raid which ended in disaster and Ivan was killed in a running battle with the Japanese.

Douglas, to his alarm, was sent on an Officer's Field Gunnery Course in Deolali. He was nervously aware that his commission was wildly unofficial and he appealed to Rowley for advice. Rowley dismissed Douglas's fears airily.

'If anyone asks you,' he said, 'say you were commissioned in the Straits Defence Forces. And get Artillery Training Volume III off by heart. You'll be the star of the course.'

Rowley reflected complacently on his ability to pick good officers.

Later in the war after service in India, Douglas was posted to a Special Forces unit and parachuted into enemy-held Malaya where he operated with the resistance movement until the Japanese surrender. Broom and Davis also returned to Malaya by submarine.

Rowley's reverie had carried him almost through the cherry orchard and he reined in when he heard the children shout.

'Cherries, sahib,' they cried, dismayed that he had not seen them.

He grinned as he reached up for the cherries and dropped them into the children's cupped hands. Twenty days to go, he thought, biting into the fruit and he planned each day and how he would spend it.

When they had eaten their fill the children ran off laughing and Rowley trotted his horse back to the hotel in pleasant anticipation of the breakfast which awaited him.

But there was a message in his pigeon-hole behind the booking clerk's desk.

He read it and cursed fluently under his breath. The clerk looked up.

'Would you prepare my bill,' said Rowley. 'I've been recalled from leave.'

The interlude was over. Ahead of him waited the jungles of Burma.

Bibliography

The Second World War, volume 4. *The Hinge of Fate*, Winston Churchill (Cassell, London)

Singapore, James Leasor (Doubleday, New York)

The Fall of Singapore, Frank Owen (Michael Joseph, London)

The War in Malaya, Lt General A. E. Percival (Eyre and Spottiswoode, London)

Four Samurai, Arthur Swinson (Hutchinson, London)

History of the Second World War, Vol. 5. (Purnell and Sons)

Singapore, Brigadier Ivan Simson (Leo Cooper Ltd.)

Who Dies Fighting, Angus Rose (Jonathan Cape, London)

The Heroes, R. McKie (Pacific Books)